Dear santa claus,

Hello, how are you I hope you're Fine I can guess you are pretty busy with all trose gifts you have to make. santa I wrote this letter to tell you that my mother cant buy me, my sister and my brother clothes or toys For christmas. she would like to make us a nice meal but she dont got money. santa we have been good this year around. santa please send us something. we are good kids. I would not like to see my sister and brother sad on christmas. send us anything you want

We love you

Love,
Santa

a different
kind of
Christmas story

Sharon Glassman

illustrations by Santiago Cohen

WARNER BOOKS

An AOL Time Warner Company

Warner Books, Inc.
1271 Avenue of the Americas
New York, NY 10020

Visit our Web site at www.twbookmark.com.

 An AOL Time Warner Company

Printed in the United States of America
First Printing: October 2002

10   9   8   7   6   5   4   3   2   1

Library of Congress Cataloging-in-Publication Data
Glassman, Sharon.
  Love, Santa : a different kind of Christmas story / Sharon Glassman.
    p. cm.
ISBN 0-446-67945-3
  1. Santa Claus. 2. Santa Claus—Correspondence. 3. Children's writings. I. Title.

GT4985 .G55 2002
394.2663—dc21   2002016809

Book design and text composition by Spinning Egg Design Group
Cover design by Brigid Pearson
Cover and interior illustrations by Santiago Cohen

*To the men and women of
Operation Santa Claus, and
Undercover Santas
everywhere.*

Acknowledgments

A huge and heartfelt thank-you to everyone who so generously gave their time, assistance, and expert advice to this book, including Vincent Camastro, Pete Fontana, Pat McGovern, Andrew Sozzi, and Diane Todd of Operation Santa Claus; Undercover Santa party hosts Beverly Coyle, Angela Jobe, Sarah Martin and her team, Janet Pines and Bill Lukashok, Paul Ward, and Joey Xanders; my infinitely creative friends Frank DeCaro, Cori Nichols, Rosemarie Ryan, Scott Wadler, and Kris Waldherr; agent *extraordinaire* Dan Mandel; editorial goddesses Amy Einhorn and Sandra Bark; and my family, for showing that giving is the best gift of all.

December 22nd, 2 A.M.

New York City is lit up like one big Christmas tree. Yellow cabs race down its arteries between green and red lights. Champagne-fueled people in shiny, tight clothes weave in and out of late-night clubs like human tinsel.

But if you want to sample the biggest holiday celebration the city has to offer—the Real Christmas Deal—you have to come here, to the all-night main Manhattan post office on Thirty-third Street and Eighth Avenue, across the street from Madison Square Garden.

Within the post office's humid, massive gray stone walls, hundreds of exhausted, frustrated—yes, even surly—citizens are only a few stamps away from true holiday satisfaction.

I know.

See that short Jewish woman with the curly red hair, the one with the alternating looks of agony and ecstasy flashing across her face? That's me. I have been waiting in line here for two overheated, fluorescent-lit hours. But every minute I spend in line brings me one step closer to my first undeniably true experience of Christmas. And I've been waiting in *that* line for twenty twisted years.

I grew up ninety miles downtown in a suburban Philadelphia family that always got visits from Santa but could never (*Oy, Gottenu!*), ever, have a Christmas tree. Torn between assimilating or isolating us from Christmas, my not exactly religious but totally culturally Jewish parents made the Solomonic choice and did a little of both.

As a result, the holiday tableau in our house rarely jibed with the ones on traditional holiday cards. Although I bet there's a thriving niche market for "bits of both" seasonal greetings in thousands of families along the CJNC—the Conservative Jewish Northeast Corridor.

Mixed-nuts imagery aside, my parents' culturally kosher Christmas offered the best of both worlds in so many ways. And, as long as I was a kid, "the best" was fine with me.

But adults are born to raise trouble. More specifically, suburban Jewish adults are born to raise trouble for themselves. Growing up, I became mildly curious, then blatantly envious, and finally, totally, histrionically obsessed with test-driving that other kind of Christmas—the kind I watched television specials about with my family for all those years, and heard friends complain about in school.

Every January, on our first day back from the vacation that was nondenominationally rechristened "winter break" between fifth and sixth grade, my Christmas-celebrating friends would trade stories of disappointing presents, infuriating siblings, infinite church services, and undeserved holiday chores from the December 25 just past. Their voices echoed the world-weary tones our fathers now use to compare cholesterol counts.

But from where I sat, one cracked green lunch tray and yet a cultural world away, the events they took for granted were filled with magic and mystery. Unremarkable suburban dining rooms were transformed into operatic halls where ducks and hams were eaten midafternoon at tables laid with multiple columns of shiny flatware. Small- to medium-sized boxes tied with colored tinsel revealed geodes, penknives, and hand-blown bottles. Bigger boxes with telltale holes brought life-altering additions to the family unit or domicile: A puppy! A piano! No, wait—a *synthesizer*!

I listened to each story, almost speechless, eyes wide with envy, mouth full of school-issue fish sticks or homemade PB&J on rye. At my house, the arrival of a living animal or piece of nondesigner furniture would mean nothing less than a total breakdown in the social and aesthetic fabric of our lives, a personal invitation to anarchy, criminal behavior, or, the ultimate enemy, dust. For kids who did Noël, these changes were just what happened between each Thanksgiving and the New Year. Definitely better than their annual trip to the dentist, but infinitely more annoying than summer camp.

As a seminormal kid, I knew better than to admit how much I envied the holiday rituals my friends derided. Instead, I listened sympathetically to their Christmas war stories, shook my head, and randomly intoned our generation's om, the singular word we used to honor an infinite range of emotional, physical, and experiential states: *bum-mer*.

But the invisible Hebrew letters in the imaginary cartoon bubble floating over my head spelled out the true story: "Bring on my first real Christmas, Rudolph," they read from right to left in blazing emotional neon. "Bring it on!"

As college in Philly gave way to a supposedly more adult stage of life in New York City, I started to think of Christmas as this supercool A-list jock, cheerleader, and conceptual artist party that everybody on the planet was invited to except me: Ms. B-list, the cute but klutzy, semi-arty loser.

3

It all seemed so simple, yet so unfair. All I wanted was to partake of the holiday spirit everyone else shared so effortlessly—pine-scented, nutmeg-flavored, eggnog-drenched. To be as one with everything that was pure Noël on my own terms. I didn't want to convert, but I didn't want to feel like some cultural anthropologist reporting on another culture's customs from the outside, either. Like a kid seized with holiday desire for a hot toy in a fake snow-frosted store window, all I wanted for Christmas every year was *Christmas*, damn it. All I wanted was a nice, bright, shiny Christmas that was MINE, MINE, MINE!

These are the noble motives that bring me here, to the main Manhattan post office during New York's prime mugging hours, up to my bruised knees in pack-ages for three kids I'll never meet, kids whose letters to Santa I took home from this very building less than a week ago.

That's when this trendy friend of mine clued me in about this thing called Operation Santa Claus, where otherwise-tough city people with holiday holes in their hearts can come down to the main post office and answer letters from kids who might not have a Christmas any other way.

A week ago, the world inside these august walls was terrifying terra incognita. Now I'm more familiar with its geography than I am with that of my apartment. I've stared at the walls for hours as I've waited in line. I've played that little game New Yorkers play when confronted with any unoccupied space larger than the hole in a pitted olive: What if I lived here? I've mentally covered the acres of postal marble floor with oversized sofas and love seats, put an imaginary industrial kitchen

4

in the alcove by the northernmost door, and thrown a housewarming party for thousands of envious, invisible guests. But ultimately, I've decided that despite its architectural grandeur—or because of it—the post office isn't the kind of place where I'd like to live, even in my dreams. I'm just your average, humble, two-bedroom condo kind of person. Or your average, humble, nineteenth-century triplex with a terrace, a garden, and an unobstructed view kind of person on a good hair day.

Depressed by the thought that I will probably never live in any of these spaces, I start looking for personally relevant messages in the government-issue slogans posted on the walls and over the doors. It's a variation on the game I play with street signs in foreign countries, or the sayings in front of local churches. I don't believe in fate, or divine omens, any more than I believe in affordable urban real estate. But I keep my eyes open, just in case some bit of eternal wisdom wants to connect with me in a down-to-earth but cosmic kind of way.

If you can believe the slogan on the banner hanging over the revolving doors: 'TIS THE SEASON TO GREET THE SPECIAL PEOPLE IN OUR LIVES. And the people in this lobby are very special indeed. The gray-haired woman on my right has just removed her dark blue loafers and hung them over her ears like two long and narrow leather muffs, possibly to filter out the scratchy choral rendition of "Silver Bells" playing on the postal PA system.

A few feet away, by the counter marked INSURED AND REGISTERED MAIL SUPPLIES, a subway conductor and bus driver in almost identical blue uniforms are voicing their heartfelt opinion that people with *real* jobs—that is, them—should be allowed—nay, required!—by law to cut in line. They pause for a second to see if anyone will let them cut ahead. Then they politely get in line with the rest of us.

It's going to be a long night, ladies and gentlemen. Trust me.

To pass more time, I peruse the flyers from other government agencies posted on the wall between each postal window. They range from creepy-spooky to truly scary. The orangy-pink FDA flyer tells me to avoid this year's most dangerous playthings, from electric bath toys to celebrity-chef dolls with tiny real knives. The malarial yellow ATF flyer asks all postal patrons to kindly leave our guns at home.

For the last half hour, I've been staring at the ceiling, where a different kind of message is spelled out in sculpted gold letters on the antique green tile panel over my head. The message, as I read it, says: DIEU ET SON DROIT. Which, if my high school French hasn't expired, means "God and His right."

If I were less delirious, I might stop to ask myself why God, if He exists, would choose to assert His rights in French on the ceiling of New York City's only twenty-four-hour post office at two o'clock in the morning. And what is God doing here anyway? We're here to mail letters, not chat with (possibly real) higher powers. But one thing I've learned these last few days of being an "undercover" Santa is that I'll take all the help I can get.

At which point, God says in a French-Canadian accent just like that of the away teams' announcers I've heard during hockey games at Madison Square Garden, across the street, "Please excuse my interruption, *mais*—but—what is this beautiful *obsession* you hold with Christmas?"

Can it be? Have I holiday-shopped myself into insanity?

"*Allô*, miss?" the voice says, from what sounds like the ceiling, thanks to the echo, but turns out to be from the guy standing right beside me in the bend of the line.

He's got a beard—brown—and a smile—white—and two very nice-looking blue eyes. He's got at his feet an official hockey stick and gym bag from the Canadian hockey team that beat the Rangers at Madison Square Garden earlier tonight. And a United States passport application in his hand.

"I have just finished my game," he says. "Now I have come here to see about my *application*." He's really working the French accent thing. And it's working. "And I see that you are—*complètement*—completely? Completely to the top with holiday spirit. All your boxes . . . your little bag of matching sweets. So nice!"

He points to the three-pound family-size holiday bag of Hershey's chocolate Kisses in red and green foil that I've been fueling myself with for the last few days like a hiker with no compass but a lot of gorp. I offer him a chocolate.

It's going to be a long night, but it's suddenly gotten a lot more interesting.

"Man, you are really talking to the wrong person if you want to talk about the joys of Christmas," I say. "I've got a tale of woe—do you know *woe*? Like misery? Pain? Right, pain! Well, I've got a tale of woe that's longer than this line. And like so many things you're not supposed to do in this country, the whole mess started with a big fat *X*."

He smiles. A French-accented, irresistible smile.

"You really want to hear about Christmas?"

"*Mais oui.* But yes! That is why I have asked."

"Okay," I say. "But before we get started, I have to tell you that the passport office here doesn't open until nine A.M. See that blue sign? The one that says passport window is open nine to five? You know, *Neuf à cinq?*"

"Thank you for showing it to me," the man says, eyes flashing, beard doing whatever it is that beards do so devastatingly well. "Now I would like to hear about Christmas. Please."

"Are you sure?" I ask.

"*Bien sûr,*" he says. "Of course. I believe, as you say, we both have all night."

✉

In the beginning, there was Charlie Brown.

Every year from the time I was old enough to sit up until I was old enough to drive, from Thanksgiving through Christmas Eve, my ethnically Jewish, pop culturally pro-Noël family and I camped out on our red-and-green-plaid living room couch to watch a month of holiday television specials.

My mom went crazy for the shows in which sports team–size families of naturally straight-haired blond people sang perky and/or reverent songs around luscious fir trees laden with gifts and red bows. During the instrumental codas, she did these totally annoying fake ballet leaps in front of the set, until we screamed at her to please—okay, pretty-please—STOP!

From preschool until college, my sister's and my number-one show, hands down, no contest, was *A Charlie Brown Christmas.* We were addicted to the

swinging sound track and the redemptive message about the lovability of little trees, and little kids, as both of us were by far the shortest kids in our class.

But Charlie Brown and the tree were just the beginning, the appetizer, the hors d'ouevre. Our December *TV Guide* was the televisual equivalent of a bag of chips: Once we'd opened it and tasted that first special, we weren't happy until we'd devoured every one.

("Speaking of snacks, would you like another holiday foil–wrapped Hershey's Kiss?" I ask Mr. Canada. "They're from the suburbs of Philadelphia, just like me." Did I really just say that? I can't believe I just said that! But he just smiles and says, "You are very kind, thank you. Yes, please.")

Every year, we booed the Grinch's selfishness and applauded his ever-expanding heart. We gave Rudolph extra credit for saying *no* to that nose job while triumphing in his chosen field, like one of our other major cultural idols, Barbra Streisand. We even watched *The Year Without a Santa Claus*, the special whose creepy villain, Heat Miser, combined with its weird style of animation, gave me recurring nightmares of being chased through an annoyingly repetitive landscape by arthritic monsters.

But every year, Frosty melted Heat Miser's heart. And every year, after two weeks of watching the singing and the snow and the never-ending stories of redemption and happiness, my family melted into a comfort and joy–infused teamlet of four height-challenged brunettes who, for a few heedless days, were as naturally, as blondly committed to the spirit of Christmas as the Williamses, the Crosbys, and platinum white Frosty himself.

One mid-December day after school, when I was ten years old and my sister five, I took her to the park around the corner to see if we could talk a lonely little tree into becoming insanely lush and beautiful, like the one on the Charlie Brown special. When that plan failed, we built a snowman, which we decided could come to life only when no one was looking. It was my first experience with the power of a creative backup plan.

That Saturday, my dad drove us across our suburb to see the Palermo family's house, a white stucco two-story that was miraculously re-created every December with thousands of dollars' worth of illuminated sleighs and reindeers and red, green, and white lights. Everybody in our corner of the greater Philadelphia area visited the Palermo house during the holiday season. It was as de rigueur as watching the feather-clad, ukulele-strumming Mummers strut through Center City on New Year's Day.

On Saturday nights, Mr. and Mrs. Palermo got dressed up as Mr. and Mrs. Claus in matching sets of his and hers white wigs, red suits, and Brooks Brothers penny loafers. As the kids lined up to talk to Santa, the adults thanked Mrs. P. for another unforgettable display and the little cup of "corrected" cocoa she offered from a silver platter. Despite our differences, all of us children—sporty and nerdy, tall and small—asked Santa for the same blessed thing at the end of our Christmas list: to make our parents as rich as Mr. Palermo, so we could have amazing lights at home next year, too.

Driving home, my mother, spirits spiked with Palermo cocoa *au rhum*, invented a new form of Christmas torture: an original medley of her favorite

Christmas carol titles, which she sang over and over again to the tune of "Jingle Bells" and ended with a calypso beat.

"Jin-gle BELLS! Sil-ent NIGHT! WE THREE Kings are— Everybody now!" My sister and I pretended to have died from shame in the backseat. Three verses later, when my mother still hadn't stopped singing, we started snoring to show her that while we were not technically dead, we were dead asleep and deserving of silence.

Two blocks later, a sonic Christmas war was raging in my dad's blue-on-blue Buick. The louder my mother sang in the front seat, the louder we snored in back. Then we added snorts and whistles, which were never as convincing as we wanted them to be, because we couldn't stop laughing. Which totally pissed us off. We didn't mean to laugh! Which was the thing that finally pulled my dad into the game.

"Does anybody hear any *snoring* back there?" he asked, looking into his rearview mirror and making this blatantly fake "I'm so confused" face, which made us laugh even more. By the time we pulled in the drive-way, everybody was crying and hiccuping, laughing so hard that my mom promised to sing even louder next year.

At this point, I've got so much holiday perfection in my life, I could have had my own family-based special: *A Very Suburban Philly Christmas,* featuring all four of us singing my mother's medley of carol titles in front of my parents' purely decorative white living room fire-place.

There was just one problem: On December 25, after weeks of holiday foreplay, and a morning spent joyfully opening the presents Santa had left for us on the second shelf of the living room armoire, next to the chrome-framed color eight-by-tens of my parents' trip to Israel, my family hopped into our car in the eerie, silent dark of early winter. We pulled out of our driveway carefully (so much snow, so many travelers!) with all the other Real Christmas families.

There was a wood-paneled station wagon filled with kids in front of us, and another one behind us. We could see them through the Christmas tree shapes we cleared with our mittens on the steamy back windows: blond parents in front, kids in back, wearing rugged jackets over sweaters like the ones we'd seen on TV.

We waved to them, and they waved back. "Merry Christmas!" We caravanned, our blue four-door between their wagons, to the main intersection of town, with its four-way stoplight and its warning written in big white letters across the black asphalt: PED. XING.

On the corners, the previous night's snow had created sloping white hills in front of the pharmacy, the bakery, the plant nursery, and the Quaker schoolhouse. Tiny fairy lights on tall leaf-free trees highlighted nature's clean peace and calm. For almost a full minute, we were silent—setting a new family record.

Normally, our suburb had none of the natural charm of a village or a town. With the exception of these four buildings from older, gentler times, our main street was just another holding zone for gas stations and discount drugstores and clothing stores with puns for names (the SWEATer SHOP, the SHOEHORN!). A mile down the road, it intersected with Route 1, the saddest way from Miami to Maine.

But that night, there was an old-world, small-town

quiet everywhere. We were at the Christmas crossroads: a place of pure holiday magic, where anything could happen. And nobody wanted to be the first person to break this holy gift of silence.

The light turned green. Our car headed left, toward our favorite Chinese restaurant. The Real Christmas kids' cars turned right, to the churchy part of town. And it hit me that this intersection marked the spot between the world of people who did Real Christmas and those of us who did Xmas, aka Christmas Lite.

"Wait a second!" I screamed.

"What? Where is it? What?" my dad yelled, braking to avoid colliding with whatever he thought I saw in the road.

"Don't yell at your father when he's driving!" my mother shouted at me when she realized there was no immediate danger. "What do you want to do, get us killed?"

My sister, terrified that she'd never be able to play with her new Christmas sled, hoop skirt–flaunting "Miss Scarlett" doll, and glow-in-the-dark poster of tropical fish if we died and went to heaven right then, began to cry.

In that moment, I realized that my family was suffering from Christmas misdirection, a spiritual condition I'd later describe to my postcollege suburban-refugee friends over too-strong black coffee and organic bitter orange marmalade muffins as "a serious case of Robert Frost meets Dante gone wrong." We had come to a dark forest—okay, a couple of trees and a stoplight—in the middle of our lives, and had chosen the road less traveled. But in this case, that was the wrong choice! I wanted us to take the well-traveled road to the churchy part of town and find out what Christmas was really about.

Get it? Get it?

That's what I used to say to my parents to make sure they got the punch lines I read to them from *My First Little Book of Big Jokes.* And it's what I kept asking them as I tried to explain my holiday revelation over our traditional Christmas dinner of spare ribs and wontons and chicken lo mein at Chun Hing Restaurant, located in the little outdoor mall ten minutes down the road.

I wanted my parents to agree that our way of doing Christmas, while wonderful, was missing something. I mean, I loved my presents and everything, I really did! Despite the fact that Santa brought me a Suzie Homemaker oven when I had asked him for an Easy Bake oven. What was Christmas missing, exactly? I didn't know. But my parents would. They were parents. Parents had to know everything.

Including why Santa had brought me a Suzie Homemaker oven.

To adults, the two toys were indistinguishable pieces of teal plastic with tiny ten-watt lightbulbs inside. But every girl on the planet knew the Easy Bake was cool, while the Suzie was for losers. On the television commercial I watched religiously every Saturday morning, Santa left the Easy Bake under the Christmas tree of a girl who looked about my age.

Seconds after this girl unwrapped her gift from Santa, there was a knock on the door: seven girls in matching pastel polyester outfits had dropped by to bake cakes! It's incredible how much power that oven had. In our suburb, pastel girls didn't talk to book-girls like me unless we had older brothers with clear skin, lanky builds, shag haircuts, and zodiac medallions that dangled on their geometrically printed, flammable synthetic shirts—or a swimming pool.

The Suzie Homemaker oven, on the other hand, was just an oven. I'm not even sure it had its own commercial. Could Santa, by giving me a Suzie, have been trying to give me a hint that I wasn't hip enough for an Easy Bake, or for groovy pastel-wearing friends?

"Santa was just extra busy this year," my mother said.

"It's an honest mistake. Perhaps he brought you some other girl's toy," my father said.

And I could almost believe it. But Christmas was for everyone, and that meant that I could have one, too. Even if I was more of a Suzie Homemaker than an Easy Bake kind of girl.

But my parents didn't get it. They just kept telling me how the Christmas season was for everybody, but Christmas was only for people who believed in Jesus. "Remember!" they said. "Today is Jesus' birthday! That's what Christmas is really about!"

Years later, I would be on a TV talk-show panel with a man who had just written a book that claimed the tradition of a late December holiday began as a seasonally based celebration to help folks get through the darkest days of winter. According to the archaeological evidence, he would say, Jesus was born in March, not December. He was an Aries! But, just as Lincoln's and Washington's birthdays got combined into the more seasonally convenient President's Weekend in the States, Jesus' birthday party got moved over the years from March to December, when people were used to celebrating the big things in life.

The whole cultural-historical explanation made so

much sense. But I wouldn't know about it for years. And besides, what are facts compared to pure emotion?

"Everybody knows that Christmas is Jesus' birthday!" I said. It's not like I'm stupid. "But what about the bigger thing?"

"What bigger thing?"

"What about the *fun*?"

"Hold on a second. Aren't we having fun?" my dad asked in that parenty way that gets the words but misses the point. "We're going to the movies after dinner. Isn't *that* fun?"

Definitely. I stole my sister's seat when she got up to go to the bathroom, and ate all my red Jujubes first.

It's just that driving home across the X in the road later that night, I looked around us for the Real Christmas families' cars, and no one's was there. We were alone in the magic, driving silently through the night as a light new snow fell. Sounds pretty perfect, doesn't it? And it would have been, if I had been any kind of normal person. Like the Real Christmas kids, or the rest of my family. But I was neither, or both. Or something in between.

That's the first time I wondered if maybe the problem with Christmas isn't other people. Maybe it's just me.

✉

Does any of this make sense to you?" I ask Mr. Canada.

"*Mais certainement,*" he says. "But certainly!"

I wonder: Could I fall in love with a man who gets hit in the face with flying plastic for a living? Could I?

"So," he says, looking adorably patient, and truly interested. "What is happening next?"

I think I could.

✉

So now it's six years and 364 days later. I was sitting in my dad's blue car, stopped by another red light at that same pedestrian crossing in the road near our house. Only this time, I was driving. I was on my way to my first real boyfriend's house for my first real Christmas Eve dinner.

Everybody knows you can't boyfriend your way into Christmas. So if you're thinking I decided to fall in love for the first time in my life with a Sicilian-American guy from a super-religious, Christmas-loving, seven-fish-courses family for any ulterior motives, you're wrong. I just cut tenth-grade algebra on the right day.

We were having a remedial quiz on binomial equations, which I hated almost as much as I hated nuclear energy plants and the whale-hunting industry. I was offended by their unnatural appropriation of parentheses and letters, which belonged in English class, the way those PROPERTY OF PHYS. ED. DEPT sweatshirts the jocks wore in the halls really belonged in the gym. I even hated the name—binomial. It sounded more like a personality disorder than a way of solving things.

On the morning of the big bino test, I rode to the park on my bike, my books clipped to the little metal shelf over the back wheel. Swinging and smoking in the early-spring suburban breeze, I waited for my parents to go to work. Then I rode home and forged a note from my mother, attributing my late arrival at school to a brief but violent case of food poisoning. I fried two eggs with provolone and hot peppers, made some raisin toast and black coffee, ate a leisurely brunch over the comic section of the morning paper, and biked to school.

As I slunk up the third-floor hallway, there he was: four ten, like me.

Staring, like me.

With a gold Saint Christopher's medal around his neck.

Like all great couples from romantic films of the forties, we immediately engaged in pithy banter to hide our true, undeniably passionate feelings.

"You dropped your sweatshirt," he said.

"Thanks, man," I said.

Then he walked into my friend Sarah's chemistry class.

We had our differences. Biz was a social, A+-list, beer-drinking fifteen-year-old whose reputation as a hands-down student and teacher favorite had been cemented during his effortlessly popular years at the junior high next door. He was friends with people who were or dated cheerleaders, played guitar in bands that signed major label deals after college, and had naturally floppy hair. Was asked to every party. Drove a stick-shift orange VW Bug with no heat. Jumped double-diamond moguls. Tanned, never burned. Got along great with my little sister, who adored him. He was amazed at how much of a brat I was, how insufferably rude I was to my parents, how dumb I was to smoke stinky cigarettes.

I was your basic introverted, hair-in-the-face, cigarette- and pot-smoking acoustic guitar freak from the junior high across town.

I marveled at Biz's 11:00 P.M. curfew, his microscopic allowance, his acceptance of going to 5:00 A.M. Mass before ski trips or crew practice, where he bossed guys twice his size to victory with a cheap burgundy megaphone attached to his head. Most of all, I admired his ability to climb out a third-story window and then drive off with the clutch of his car disengaged once his parents went to bed, assured by his angel face in their bedroom doorway that he was, as always, safely at home on time.

His lips were almost always chapped. He was going to be a doctor for kids with life-threatening diseases: I was going to be . . . well, you know, something cool. We would get married when he got out of med school.

During our second December together, Biz's mother graciously invited me over for Christmas dinner. After dinner, we are *all* going to go to midnight Mass. Good-bye, evil *X* in the road. Hello, Christmas!

On the afternoon of what I was hoping would be my first real Noël, I took a bath, not a shower. I hated baths, but they took longer, and I'd recently developed this formula: The longer something takes to get ready for, the more life-altering it could be. I didn't wear makeup yet, so I shaved my legs twice to kill more time.

If this had been an ordinary night in a warmer season, I would have ridden my bike to Biz's house, humming the Joni Mitchell song of angst and longing I'd worked out on my acoustic guitar that afternoon.

Barefoot, bike basket filled with tulips and daisies, dressed in what a teen fashion magazine might have called my "highly personal style" of multiple flowered skirts with layers of lacy blouses tied on top, I would not be just another confused sixteen-year-old on a dark blue three-speed with foot brakes. I'd be Arty Bike Girl! Insulated from the stares of the cool high school girls with their huge hoop earrings and pastel satin bomber jackets. Able to leap through jock parties in a single bound.

But even Arty Bike Girl was no match for Christmas. So I pulled out my ultimate weapon: a long velveteen dress with a high white lace collar and petticoat, which I thought was so nineteenth century, but which people on the bus must have thought was some kind of teenage maternity frock. They always tried to give me their seats when I wore it to go to the mall in Center City to chain-smoke with my friends in the Food Court.

But there will be no smoking tonight, young lady, my more serious Christmas self told my rebellious self sternly. No lace vests tied over the velveteen. Instead, I pulled my frizzy henna-colored hair into a tight bun off-set with "tendrils," which now, with fashion hindsight, I realize must have looked more like fuzzy strands of hair pulled loose on each side. As I pulled my dad's car out of the driveway, I had transformed Arty Bike Girl into her more elegant and polite alter ego. I had become Lace-Clad Girlfriend of Christmas!

And when the light turned green in front of the *X* in the road, I turned right, toward the churchy part of town!

Biz's house was beautifully lighted with little electric candles. The candlelight emphasized the brick and stone walls and the little porch with its neatly piled cord of wood. The wreath on the door was made of fresh wreathy things and studded with berries. I'd never dined in a house with a wreath on the door before! I straightened my skirt. I breathed in deeply. I rang the bell, which did not chime the melody to "Ave Maria," as I had hoped. (Hey, you can't have everything.)

Biz answered the door, decked out in his yellow corduroy blazer, lightly flared chocolate brown trousers, and knit tie. He was beautiful.

Inside, opera singers were discreetly murmuring carols on his father's living room stereo. OoOOOooo

HoOOOooly Ni-i-ight! Firelight illumined the tree—the *tree*!—which was elegantly decorated in ornaments selected by Biz's sisters, Lissie and Claudia, and his brother, Andrew.

I handed Biz's dad the bottle of wine my dad had bought him and gave his mom a box of cookies my mom had bought her. Then I sat down at my designated place at the table: next to Claudia and across from Biz. This was a dinner with rules. We really could have been in the nineteenth century!

As Biz's dad said grace, my family, two and a half miles and a cultural world away, was gathering around the television—our annual holiday tableau. They would watch the same Christmas Eve specials we'd watched together every year. They would eat the grilled cheese sandwiches and canned tomato soup my mom would heat up as part of her annual display of home cooking, because "None of the pizza places are open tonight and, let's face it, folks, who wants to eat Chinese food two nights in a row?" Tonight, of course, there would be one less cheese sandwich to grill. Our teamlet was no longer four persons strong, but three. Of course, any pangs I had about breaking tradition had been overwhelmed by the joys of becoming a Real Christmas person. But my parents, my sister—how would they deal with the pain?

In my moment of silent reflection, I saw my sister spread out across the empty space on the right side of the couch, the place that had—Hey! Get off of that!—always been mine. My mother was helping herself to my share of the iced sugar cookies shaped like little Santa hats. My father was asking her to bring him a diet soda.

"Amen!" said Biz's entire family.

"Amen," I echoed. Let it be.

And then it was time to go around the table and repeat the introductions we'd done earlier in the foyer. I quickly forgot the old battles at home. Christmas now meant so many new faces and so many new names!

There were Nonno and Nonna, and Nonno and Nonna number two. There were "the aunts," Biz's father's sisters, who lived together as a team. And then there were Biz's mother's sisters, who had brought their husbands and their kids. I waved to the ones I recognized from school; they were sitting at the other end of the block-long all-wood dining table, trying to switch their water glasses for their parents' full glasses of wine.

The sideboard behind them was covered with steaming tureens. And if that wasn't enough of a hint about the upcoming holiday feast, the English library–style red silk walls were covered with pictures of things that were or could be edible once they were no longer alive. There were fruits, and rabbits—poor rabbits—and fish with their Latin names drawn underneath their portraits. Over the next three hours, seven courses of real fish were brought to the table: *baccalà*, salty and pungent, sweet *branzino* in butter, *trota* in white wine, and *scungil'* bathed in garlic, which I was convinced should be sold as a perfume. (Okay, maybe not.)

I said no to all the fish courses—I was a vegetarian at this point; still am. But then aunt number three, who had been a nurse in World War II, brought out the pasta. Each aunt had her own dish and, not to hurt anybody's feelings, the family had asked the aunts to cook them all, twice. There were shells with cheeses, and noodles with spicy red sauce . . .

"You want more?" asked aunt number one, who had the kindest smile I'd ever seen. "What's your name? Someone tell me this little girl's name! Whom do you belong to?"

"She's all mine, *Zia!*" Biz said.

"Eric!" his mother said, and Biz, whose parents ignored his nickname entirely, hung his head.

"Sure," I said. "I'll have more!"

"Have some more," aunt number two, the gardener, said five minutes later, which was about four minutes too soon.

"Sure, okay. A little more!"

"Just two noodles more," said aunt number three. "*Due spaghettini!*"

Please, God, no. Biz kicked me under the table. "Yes, please!"

"Aha!" said aunt number four—whom Biz's dad called "the almost Jewish one" for her skills with guilt—as I pushed a slab of pasta the size of my head around my plate. "You eat her lasagna *twice,* and you don't touch mine?"

It was exactly the way I'd always imagined my first true Christmas would be. Then at ten o'clock, while the rest of the family and I were discussing which of the aunts' cakes we should try first, Biz said, "I think I'm gonna go upstairs a second."

As my true beloved headed upstairs, I took a break from being Lace-Clad Girlfriend of Christmas, so I could worry about what was going to happen at church. I wasn't really scared that anyone was going to do anything too New Testament, like crucify or beatify anybody. But I had never been to a church service before. And I was sure it was going to change me in some profound and fundamental way. The only question was, How?

It was a question with long-term implications. I hated binomials, but I loved geometric proofs. In my mind, it went like this:

IF Biz and I are madly in love (which we are)

AND planning on getting married (although that's our secret for now),

AND IF Biz is Catholic,

AND we're going to church together,

THEREFORE, isn't going to church a next step on the road to getting married? And by inviting me here—and letting me go—don't both sets of our parents agree?

To put it more simply: Biz+Me+Midnight Mass = the 2 of Us 4 Ever.

The only question that remained was, What was I going to do while everybody else knelt? Kneeling, I knew from ten years of Hebrew School, was number one on the list of Jewish no-no's, even for those of us raised on grilled cheese with bacon.

Fortunately, I wasn't religious. Then suddenly— maybe it was the wine, or the secondhand exposure to all seven Christmas fishes in one night—I was not only worried about whether God existed; I was terrified that His plan for that evening was to watch me walk into church at 11:59. If I knelt, I'd be smoted. (Smited? Smitten? Smelt?) If I didn't kneel, how rude would that be to my future family-in-law?

I was dreaming up a demikneel, something that God, if He turned out to be Jewish, might forgive as a curtsy if I asked hard enough next Yom Kippur, when we heard Biz throwing up his guts in the guest bathroom. I got up to help, only to find myself eighth or ninth in line behind every female in his family.

"Sit down!" Biz's dad said. I sat down—fast. "Everything's all right, everybody. Eric, are you all right?"

Ten-fifteen: Biz was still upstairs. Aunts were running up and down the stairs with cold towels. Those of us left at the table passed the time folding and unfolding our napkins. The official verdict was: Flu.

At 10:45, I drove home. No one was going to Mass that night. At home, my parents were worried about Biz, but relieved to see no stigmata on my hands.

The score was now official. Christmas: 2. Me: 0.

✉

Mr. Canada, potential father of my potential future children, smiles. He always smiles. Maybe it's a Canadian pro-hockey habit. A way to reassure me he still has all his teeth.

"More chocolate?" I say.

"Not now. Thank you, no."

Up ahead of us, the postal line is moving at a less-than-glacial pace, which makes me very happy indeed.

My new holiday motto, the one I've lovingly hand-crafted to go with the game of Flirt I'm playing with Mr. Handsome Canadian, is: Less pace in line, more time with you know who.

"The score is Christmas two and you have zero," he says.

"And it stayed that way for the next ten years."

"That is not fair!"

"Tell me about it! Then I ended up in another blue car, but not my father's blue car."

"In Philadelphia!" Mr. Canada tries to score a point, and . . . misses!

"Actually, it was in Rome." A look of surprise crosses his sensitive but manly features.

"Are you there . . . alone?" he asks, clearing the way for me to reach my goal of seeing if he looks jealous when I say:

"Um. Well. Actually, there was a guy in the car." Can he handle the blow? Will he let down his defenses and let his true feelings for me show?

"Tell me more!" my pro athlete says bravely.

Our little game has produced a shutout. For now.

✉

So I was driving another blue car—a stick shift this time, so I was driving pretty slowly—on a mountain road outside of Rome. No X-ing in the road, but it was, yes, Christmas Eve—*la vigilia*. The Wait.

After years of American disappointments, I had been invited to celebrate Christmas in the most romantic city in the world by the most transcendently handsome man I had ever met. A six-foot-one, blond, blue-eyed Roman god named Tommaso—Tomi, for short.

We'd met on a train five years before, when I took a summer off to travel through Europe. I spoke less than ten words of Italian then. Tomi had only started studying English in school that spring. But as the Italian Alps passed by our train window, we shared a look that said so much more than words ever could.

For the next five years, Tomi wooed me with postcards filled with Italian poetry—like this: "*Tu sei la prima per me; l'ultima . . .*" "You are my first, my last . . ."

It was all so *romantico*!

It took us half a decade to hook up for a second date. Tomi was busy with school; I had my job. But then, thanks to the strength of the dollar, our passion, and the appeal of being three thousand miles away from America during Christmas, I accepted Tomi's annual invitation to join him in Rome for Christmas—*Natale* in Italian. The Birth.

As day turned into my first Italian Christmas Eve, all I could think was, Why didn't I think of this before? The scenery was stunning, and so was my date. There was an overwhelming sense of expectation in the air, and it went so much deeper than anything I'd ever felt at home. It was a two-thousand-year-old party, and every-one was invited, including me.

Tomi picked me up at my *pensione,* resplendent in his blue cashmere jacket, gray turtleneck, gray wool trousers, and elegant black leather shoes. He told me I was *bellissima*—("so very beautiful")—and who was I to disagree? I was on the road to paradise: My first real Christmas and my first real Christmas nooky, all in one night.

After a delicious dinner in a small café, Tomi led me to a fourteenth-century white stone church on the top of a hill. We walked under the stars through these perfect rows of cypress trees and then into the church, where his rugged cheekbones cast rugged shadows against the ancient candlelit walls.

At five minutes to midnight, the choir began to sing—in Latin! My first real Christmas was just ahead of me. Beside me was a Roman-nosed Adonis worthy of being in an art history book or on the cover of a men's fashion magazine. This was what I'd been waiting for. This was the fulfillment of all my Christmas dreams.

Which was when Tomi leaned over to me and

passionately whispered, "Stayin' alive! Stayin' alive! I am feeling groovy!"

It's the Euroversion of my mother and her medley of Christmas carol titles.

The choir continued to sing in Latin, but all I could hear was Tomi as he recited American pop tunes of the last twenty years—the subject of his college thesis—in my ear. He wanted to know if I could correct his pronunciation: Was it the Be-GEES or the BEE-gees? He was going to teach a course in U.S. pop classics at a local high school the following year, after he got his degree. His all-time favorite band was the Blues Brothers.

As I leaned against one of Tomi's broad cashmere shoulders and gazed up at his contented face, the site of so much expected comfort and joy, the truth about my Christmas wishes up until then shone as clearly as the stars above: My problem with Christmas had nothing to do with other people. It really just had to do with me.

✉

What a shame!" Mr. Canada says, grinning—make that openly laughing—perhaps at his potential rival's defeat.

"Hey," I say. "The good stuff's always worth waiting for." Wink, wink.

Pause. Nothing.

"And now you're here," my hockey pro says, pointing to the red-and-green-plaid down jacket I've got tied around my waist, "dressing like a Christmas tree. Or elf. Did you receive a call from Monsieur Santa Claus himself?"

Like a macho game-show spokesmodel, he raises and drops his hand and arm in the air to draw attention to the rest of my ensemble—and his biceps, bulging beneath the fabric of his official team jacket. I haven't thought much about what I've been wearing for the last few days. But as it turns out, I'm decked out in a pair of dark green pants and a red sweater that has little pieces of gold and silver wrapping foil stuck to it in dozens of places. When I pull out my makeup mirror, I also see that I've been standing here for the last several hours with foil stuck to my face and in my hair.

I look like I've been working overtime on Santa's assembly line, which, in a way, I have.

"Actually," I say, "it was a letter." We both looked down at the pile of boxes I'm mailing. They have pieces of cutout candy-cane designs on them and heart shapes and snowpeople on the front.

I can feel myself smiling.

"Okay," I say. "Actually, three letters."

The year after my Roman holiday, I spent the entire month of December in silent meditation at a mountain-top ashram, where I obsessed about you know what for all 1,440 minutes of all thirty-one days, and couldn't tell anybody how miserable I was.

A few years after that, I joined the Unitarian church around the corner from my apartment in Brooklyn. We celebrated every festive winter date on the international calendar with equal amounts of intensity, good feeling, and decaf coffee served from the Urn of Community. Which was great, really great—if you're the kind of person who likes to play the holiday field, emotionally (and sing "Kumbaya" seriously). But all I wanted was a one-on-one commitment.

Finally, I made peace with the fact that while I'd never be, you know, *merry* from November through January, the worst years of my Christmas-craving life were definitely over.

Then this year, a couple of weeks after that harbinger of hell known as Black Friday—the day after Thanksgiving, first day of the holiday shopping season—I was taking an innocent, fat-busting walk in my neighborhood to work off some holiday-related high-carb meal. I strolled past the shoe store, the card store, and the Yuppie deli. Then I came to one of those Chinese restaurants with a folding blackboard sign out front. On the sign, it said WE HAVE WARM SPINACH.

And there was something about those words—WARM SPINACH—that made me start to mist. I'm a New York woman. I don't cry. I mist! Right there in the Brooklyn autumn twilight. Because looking through the window of that restaurant, all I could imagine was this enormous group of people who'd be sitting around this huge table later that night, *gathering* around the warm spinach. And I knew Christmas was coming.

And it was headed my way: undeniably, unavoidably, stronger than it had ever been before. Because by now, everyone I'd known since we were kids had made their childhood dreams come true and moved on to bigger things. The guy who'd been concertmaster of our high school orchestra now played with the Berlin Symphony. My friend Becky from elementary school, who wanted to be an American Indian instead of a Reform Jew when she grew up, now lived on a reservation, where she had four kids and a GED. How am I ever going to grow up if I can't get past Christmas? I thought.

I decided to take control of Noël for a change, instead of waiting for it to deliver itself to me. But how?

✉

That's when my trendy friend Tina, an NYC A-lister if there ever was one, called to tell me how she'd heard about this thing called Operation Santa Claus, where you could go down to the main post office and pick up a letter from a kid who might not have a Christmas any other way.

"It's not cool, exactly," she said. "But it made me think of you. Ta-ta! Kisses! Bye!"

As I put down the phone, an idea hit me (along with a vague urge to pop Tina one for being so—*Ta-ta!*— condescending while being so infuriatingly, A-listily right). This Operation Santa Claus thing is not just the way for me finally to have my first real Christmas, I thought. I can get a little *tzedaka* in there, as well!

Tzedaka was this concept I had learned about in Hebrew school but had forgotten about until just then. It means charity—and anonymous giving of that charity, ideally. That way, the person getting the gift doesn't feel obligated to the person who gave it to them. And the person who gives the gift can be sure their motives are pure—that they're not looking for the world's biggest thank-you.

A pure Christmas? I liked the sound of this Operation Santa thing already.

The next afternoon, I took the subway to the main post office, on my way home from a meeting. Like the true, overscheduled professional that I am (or at least imitate from nine to nine), I had this entire Christmas *tzedaka* project mapped out clearly in my head. I was

going to walk up to the Operation Santa Claus window, say, "Hello. I'm here for my letter!" go home, make dinner, and get on with the rest of my life.

The only problem was, I was scared to walk in. I was standing across the street, by the back wall of Madison Square Garden, watching the sign change from WALK to DON'T WALK and back again.

Some people are afraid of serious heights. Other people are afraid of serious romantic commitments, or exotic diseases. I'm afraid of serious architecture. I get queasy every time I have to walk into a really important-looking building. I'm convinced a security guard's going to walk over and demand a ticket or a permission slip I haven't got. "There's serious adult business to be done here, miss," he'll say, with the emphasis on *adult*. Which just so isn't me. Adult? Please. I'm shocked when the kid behind the counter doesn't sell me an "under twelve" ticket at the movies.

From where I was standing, the post office was most definitely an "adult business only" building—the kind of place that would look right at home in ancient Greece or Rome. As big as a museum, as stern as a library, and as out of my league as a private bank. Two city blocks long, and an entire avenue deep. Twenty columns—I counted them twice to avoid crossing the street—connect the stairs to the roof with big stone leaves (as if the architect believed a dash of flora would convince us that entrusting our most sacred mailable items to strangers is a natural thing).

Above the southernmost columns are the words *Louis XIV in MCCCCXIV created the Poste Royale Jan Turvis Imperial Guardian*, followed by the PO mantra, literally engraved in stone in a very serious font: *Neither snow*

*nor rain nor heat nor gloom of night stays these couriers
from the swift completion of their appointed rounds.*

Gloom? Did somebody mention gloom?

Get a grip! I told myself. It's just a post office.
You've traveled the world—well, at least you took a
train around Europe. I took a deep, meditative breath,
trying to convince myself that maybe the main PO was
just a bigger version of my high school, another stone
building with seriously adult words etched above the
door. *Enter to Learn. Go Forth to Serve.*

The light turned green.

Maybe, just like high school, the main PO was an
important-*looking* building, with nothing much going on
inside.

I crossed the street.

I quickly discovered that, just like at my high
school, the steps of the main post office are where people go to smoke and scream. Two blond women in black
leather coats examined the white tips of their French-
manicured nails for unsightly nicks as they puffed blue
smoke into the gray air; a man with a matching red face
and tie told someone named Trevor Damn It to Hell by
cell phone that he'd better "find those back taxes, fast!"
They were middle-age versions of the cheerleaders and
jocks from high school. Overgrown seventeen-year-olds.

I can do this, I told myself.

As I walked up the wide granite stairs, I was a
pilgrim on the path to postal enlightenment. The gleam-
ing revolving brass doors at the top whispered to me
that the true peace of Christmas awaited me on their
other side.

Then, once I was safely inside, they screamed,
SUCK-ER!

On the postal side of the brass were hundreds of rage-propelled people who needed something *important* done *now*!

Not only that. There was no Operation Santa Claus window. Instead, there was an entire Operation Santa Claus room, packed with people who normally wouldn't be caught dead hanging out with one another. The tables on the left side of the room were filled with slick-haired business guys dressed in striped suits and thin raincoats that couldn't possibly keep them warm. The tables on the right belonged to a bunch of tough old ladies, the kind who love dogs and babies but can't stand people.

The business guys jiggled their arms and legs up and down in nervous patterns, as if they had personal stock market ticker tapes twitching under their skin. The old ladies wore brutally patient smiles that said that whatever happened next couldn't surprise them. They had seen it—whatever *it* was—a million times worse before.

The space between these two opposing camps was occupied by a gaggle of giggling high school girls wearing color-coordinated jackets and carrying knapsacks weighed down with candy-colored key chains, hairbrushes, and lip glosses in small clear tubes dangling from their zipper tabs. They'd colonized an empty patch of post office wall, piling it high with shopping bags from the mall around the corner, where smoking was now forbidden. Not that any of them smoked, judging from their healthy complexions and energy bars.

Smokers or not, it was reassuring to see that teenage girls still came in the same basic varieties they did when I hung out in malls. There was the shy girl in the light blue jacket, hiding her face behind a letter; the popular girl in the center, not doing much of anything, just glowing in that way that said she was admired. There were the best friends, who ended every sentence with "If that's okay with you!" The short girl with a rainbow of hoop earrings in one ear that matched the ends of her hair; the gawky girl, who I hoped would grow up to be anything but a model. There was the skinny girl with the open, sweet grin, and the heavy girl with the totally groovy green sweater.

Maybe it was the post office lighting, but every girl's advantage shone. And then one of them put her hand to her mouth, pointed to her letter, and said, "Oh my God, did you see that?" and "Oh my God, did you see that?"

Because in the center of the room was this enormous banquet table with seven boxes of letters on it. There was one box for each of the five boroughs of New York City and a box that said "New York State" and a box that said "Foreign."

And all of the people piled into this room as if it were a rush-hour subway car—the suits and the scary grandmas and the high school girls—were putting their hands in the boxes, pulling out a letter, saying, "Oh my God, did you see that?"

As soon as I saw an inch of free space, I ran up and put my hand into the box that said "Brooklyn," because I'd lived in Brooklyn for the last seven years. I knew the people in my building. I knew the people on the street. Sometimes, I even smiled at little kids on the sidewalk. We were all kind of connected, like family.

The second my hand touched the box, this feeling started racing up my elbow, like there was one letter that was singing to me on some kind of personal frequency. The way a red chenille sweater will sing to me from a store window when I'm just walking by, minding my own business, and I'll have to stop what I'm doing and walk right in. Only I couldn't figure out which letter was singing to me because the box was really tall, and I'm not.

I pulled my hand out of the box. It was attached to this pile of letters. I read the first one. It said: *"Dear Santa. I am the mother of an eleven-year-old boy who has been a very good boy this year, and all he would like for Christmas is something to play football with, or fish."*

How hard could that be? I figured they probably sold footballs at the corner hot dog stands, this close to Madison Square Garden! What an easy request to fulfill! And so affordable, too. I put the letter in my pocket. That was simple!

Actually, it was *too* simple.

Christmas, the full-bodied, genuine, carol-inspiring kind, as I know all too well from a lifetime of anguishing personal experience, does not happen to someone like me for answering one simple letter involving a rod, reel, and a small sports ball. Remember the *X* in the road? Rome? The ashram? I get it now. That first letter was a *tzedaka* test. A Christmas quiz. A minitrap. But you can't fool me! Expecting a true Christmas experience from answering one little letter would be like skipping one dessert and expecting to wake up with totally flat abs in the morning. That stuff only happens in dreams, and low-fat dessert commercials. Back here in the real world, one little letter couldn't change my Christmas karma.

But *two* letters could!

I hereby propose and pass the following revision to my original plan: I will look for one more letter, one that can increase my giving burden to acceptable proportions. One that will harmonize with the one that's sung its way so sweetly into my pocket. All in favor? I. Me. Whatever. This mental meeting is adjourned!

The second letter in my hand was from a boy who stapled a picture of this yellow-and-orange castle from a toy catalog onto a piece of notebook paper. And it said: *"Dear Santa: I will be happy if you bring me just this castle for Christmas. But if you bring me a different toy, that would be okay, too. I will leave your cookies in the same place as last year."*

I could resist that.

"PS: I love you, Santa."

Oh sweet Jesus, Krishna, and Jehovah, no I couldn't. *"I love you, Santa"*? This little kid I'd never seen had written four little words at the end of his letter and I was devastated: *"I love you, Santa"*? Santa, as I remembered him, was not an "I love you" kind of guy. He was more like a one-on-one corporation with a simple contract. You be good. I'll bring the presents. And now here was this kid writing *"I love you"* to a total stranger—me—who he probably thought was wearing a red polyester suit and a beard!

I walk around all day in these meticulous casual ensembles from SoHo and I'm lucky if somebody on the street says: "Nice red chenille sweater, baby!" ("Thanks, it just sang to me from a store window!") And now this little kid was offering me love—and cookies—in exchange for a plastic toy castle in the mail. I put the second kid's letter in my pocket. There was no way I was going to give up on somebody this accepting.

I had two letters now: one filled with love, one filled with ease. It was almost enough. But not really. Let's go for letter number three, I thought, and make this a holy, whole epistolary trinity!

My third letter was written by hand in all caps by an unemployed mother looking for *"A FIRST DOWN JACKET FOR MY DAUGHTER, SIZE 10/11 SMALL, IN BLACK."*

And there's something about those words—*"A FIRST DOWN JACKET"*—that made me mist in the middle of the main post office on a Thursday afternoon. Because a kid who doesn't get a football or a castle for Christmas is unhappy. But a little girl who doesn't have a down jacket to wear outside when it's cold is COLD! And that is not an acceptable thing.

The idea that there was a little girl in my borough who was cold made me want to say to everybody standing in line at the main post office, Hey you guys! There's a little girl who is freezing at this address out in Brooklyn! And in my mind, I saw everyone in the post office stop what they were doing. They put their stamps back on the counter and handed back their registered mail so we could start an organization called Friends of Post Office Kids Without Heat—FOPOKWOH, for short. We formed a conga line of righteous people and danced our way out of the main post office onto Eighth Avenue, adding people along the way. By the time we crossed the Brooklyn Bridge, there were 7 million of us, carrying safe space heaters and blankets and money to pay for gas.

So, there I was, standing at the checkout counter of Operation Santa Claus with my three letters in hand and seven boxes of runners-up behind me. I know, I told you I was looking for the one letter that would sing to me. One letter, one kid: a logical move for someone who'd never changed a diaper. But with three, I had a major chord—a family's worth of kids to whom I could give a real Christmas!

And besides, how could I possibly have put one of these letters back? Which one would I have chosen? Each letter was as personal as a child's face. How could I have looked at that face and said, "Sorry, adorable Football Boy, your request is too simple." Or "Sorry, Young Mr. Love and Cookies, there's no room for you at my one-bedroom Brooklyn inn!" How could I have listened to a letter sing and then said, "Thanks, but no thanks!" That would have made for one heartwarming image for a Christmas special, no? A Very New York Scrooge-Ass Christmas! I can just see it now:

"Please?" asks the letter, played by the voice of a compellingly real child actor. "Look. I even made a couple of cute misspellings, not the fake ones you see on Christmas specials. Actual errors, 'cause I'm a real kid. See? I even used the word—'cause—the way real kids do!"

"Sorry," says the coldhearted woman, cruelly being played by me, dressed in a month's rent's worth of new designer separates. "I know this seems hard for you, having me put you back in that overcrowded box where no one may ever hear you sing again. And yes, it's true: You could end up being recycled or something when nobody ever reads you again or takes you home. And yes, maybe on Christmas Day, instead of getting a present, the hope-filled child who wrote you will get nothing but a broken heart and a loss of faith in Santa, and, to extrapolate reasonably, humanity. And, okay, maybe that loss of faith will KO his hope of anything good happening in his life. And sure, all kids deserve to have something good happen to them, not just once in a lifetime, but once a day, like some kind of happiness vitamin.

"But hey! Look on the bright side! Maybe you'll end up with one of those guys in the suits. They may have less time than I do to shop, but, God knows, they've got more disposable cash. And isn't that what the holiday season is about? More cash, more toys, more loot? . . ."

Sorry, folks, but I had no intention of starring in that particular special. Three Christmas survivors had believed in Santa—and ended up with me, a woman who has been known to buy two nearly identical orange lipsticks just in case one of them looked a tiny bit better in natural light.

How could I have returned a letter? It would have been like returning a kid.

I was riding the subway back to Brooklyn, my letters in my Italian designer knapsack. I think I felt the way a guy must feel when he's got an engagement ring in his pocket—like everybody had to know what I was carrying, because the letters in my knapsack were singing so loudly. But everyone just minded his own business.

The first thing I did when I got home was unpack my letters and put them on top of my desk so they could breathe. Then I steamed some spinach in a warm filtered-water mist, read a book, and went to sleep. Then at four o'clock the next morning, I woke up in a cold sweat. I had gone from being an independent single woman to being the sole provider of Christmas for three innocent children. What had I been thinking?

I went running into my living room, and there they

were: three letters. Three little kids' worth of Christmases sitting on my desk. Three sets of little kid eyes looking up at me saying, We know you'll do it, Santa!

And what they were looking at right then was the worst side of myself. The scared and selfish side, which was saying, Santa, who? There is no Santa here! I am just a confused young woman in search of her first Christmas. I'm in need of help, not a provider of it!

My scary selfish side was deeply convinced there'd been a mistake, a case of confused identities. Just like when the guy behind the counter at the doughnut store calls me "Ma'am" and there's no one in the store except for him and me. I want to say, Who do you think you're talking to, young man? There's nobody grown-up here!

Three hours later, as the sun came up over Brooklyn, I was still standing there staring at those letters. I was thinking that maybe if I stared at them hard enough, I'd find a way to make this project dealable, palatable, easier to swallow.

Sure, I wanted to do good, but this much good? Why had I jumped into the deep end of the *tzedaka* pool before finding out if I could swim?

After all, I'd never done this before. Maybe I didn't have the required skills to be hired for this nonpaying but crucial job! Maybe there was some night-school course in Christmas Giving that I could take. A tutor I could hire. Maybe there were more proactive, perhaps battery-powered letters to Santa that shop for themselves?

Was it possible? Could I *fail* at the fine art of giving? Not possible! I told myself I live in a city where hailing a cab to get to work every morning requires the tactical skill of a military general and the seductive charms of a sorceress. I am equal to any of life's challenges!

Except perhaps this.

Inhale . . . exhale . . . *Get a grip!* I experienced an unexpected moment of holiday enlightenment. If this is the true, evil spirit of Christmas, I will exorcise it ASAP. I will do my Operation Santa shopping this week! Today! *This morning!* So I can get on with the rest of my life after lunch. I felt a moment of inner peace.

Then I realized, I now have to think of a place to get some deeply anonymous giving done *fast*! Near my home! So I won't die making the trip!

I had a vision—not a spiritual vision, but more like a memory with a visual snapshot attached to it. I remembered that there was a mall in my neighborhood that someone had pointed out to me once as being the mall with the "largest number of items sold per square foot in America." I saw its image in my mind's eye: gray and big and crumbling, filled with chain stores and discount stores with forgettable names.

Which was exactly why I never went there. How can you find something that sings in a place where everything looks the same? Not that I don't have a firm grip on my identity, but I have to admit I was a little bit afraid that I could walk into that mall as this serious vegetarian who shops in SoHo—east of Lafayette Street—and walk out on the other end as Arty Bike Girl, the suburban sixteen-year-old I used to be when I went shopping in malls.

As the sun feebly broke through the mid-December clouds, exchanging the hopeless black of night for a rare bright blue day, I went for a run over the Brooklyn Bridge. That's what I do when I feel like I need to be moving ahead but I don't know where I'm going. The sight of downtown Manhattan's tall buildings coming through the pointed arches always puts things in perspective. It's as if the soul of the engineer who built the bridge is saying, Hey, I figured out how to span a river with wire and a few pounds of cement. Your problem's got to be easier than that!

I was getting my first good look at the Manhattan skyline when it hit me: There was this other mall in Brooklyn.

My neighbor Rita and I had literally run into it the week before when we were looking for the parking lot we used to cut through. It was like that old Joni Mitchell song about paradise and the parking lot, only in reverse. Because where our parking lot used to be, someone had built this brand-new three-story white concrete mall with a sporting-goods store and an office-supply store. And music. We weren't just hearing music, it was singing in our bones.

The music carried us up the escalator to the second floor and dropped us off in front of this "spiritual brass band" from Harlem, which was playing at the mall because it was opening day, and anyone who was anyone in Brooklyn was there. There were grandmothers and fathers and kids who were friends and my neighbor Rita and I, all trying to see what the excitement was about.

No one went into the stores. We just stood there watching these six guys playing these jazzy versions of "Santa Claus Is Coming to Town" and "Good King Wenceslas" on the trombone. The youngest guy was about ten. The oldest was around eighty.

As the music filled the space over our heads, everybody started singing and dancing. Soon, it was a call and response, the dancing firing up the musicians to improvise riffs on carols that threatened to tear the brand-new roof off the house.

"He's the King!" the youngest trombone player shouted in a high, determined voice.

"Comin' to town!" shouted the oldest player, taking a breath-break from his horn.

As far as the crowd was concerned, the King was already there, and doing fine. People yelled "Hallelujah!" in front of T. J. Maxx and shook hands with one another. Rita and I shook hands with everyone. I was shaking. I had tears in my eyes because the music was just everywhere. The trombones were getting louder and louder. And then somebody in the crowd testified from sheer joy: "Praise the Lord—He's in the building!"

Which made sense. Why shouldn't God be celebrating the new mall with everybody else in Brooklyn?

Now, the spirit of God or Santa or modern commercial real estate was sending me back across the Brooklyn Bridge to my apartment, where I got ready to head to the new mall, where my kids' Christmas wishes would hopefully come true. I took a quick shower; packed my knapsack: Two energy bars. Check! Two lipsticks. Check, check! Checkbook. Double check! A bottle of water. An extra pair of socks in case I got blisters from shopping.

I locked the door behind me. Opened it again. Went back in and, this time, remembered to take the letters with me.

Thirty minutes later, I got off the subway at the mall in my green reversible down jacket with the red-and-green-plaid lining. It wasn't the most fashion-conscious piece of clothing I owned. Okay, in fact, it had been sitting in the back of my closet for years, but I was hoping its color scheme would bring me good Christmas luck.

As I was riding the escalator to the second floor, I passed other mothers going up to the third floor or down to the basement. Some of them were wearing down jackets. Others were holding bottles of water. We smiled. Then the other mothers looked down to make sure their kids were where they should be. And I looked in my pocket to make sure my kids—my letters—were where they were supposed to be, too.

I was sweating; I was nervous. I thought I was passing. I was an "undercover mother." The only person who knew I had *no* idea what I was doing was me.

The escalator left me off on the second floor, in front of a store that looked like the perfect place to buy a kid a castle. There were all these posters in the window of kids wearing sweatshirts with dragons on them and little denim jackets with choo-choo trains running up the sleeves. As I walked through the door, my inner sixteen-year-old Arty Bike Girl started screaming, Oh my God! That orange jumpsuit with the balloons painted on it would look great on us in an extra large! But my Undercover Mother told her, Young lady, we are not here to shop for you!

So I walked up to the security guard and said, "I'm looking for a toy castle for my, uh—"

Hold on. For this to be true Christmas *tzedaka*, the guy couldn't know I was answering these kids' letters as an act of charity. To be a *tzedaka* Santa, I needed him to think I was just another mom—the kind who knows about kids, and has them.

"For my, uh, son?"

And would you look at that! The security guard gave me this totally nonthreatening dad-to-mom smile, the kind I'd never gotten from a man in this city before. Probably because I'd never been anybody's mother before.

"Isn't it the darndest thing?" he said. "We've got windows filled with pictures of kids wearing clothes with pictures of toys on them. Then folks walk in and find out that there are no toys to buy. I told the people who run this place, 'Not that it's any of my business, but don't you think customers will find this confusing? Toys on clothes in the window. No toys inside?'

"They told me, 'It's a new "marketing concept."' Which, as far as I can see, just means, 'Ain't got a clue.' But those *marketing* people figure folks will just give in and buy something if they can be tricked into walking through the door."

This was probably a bad time to confess I earned my living in the field of marketing; that I was paid handsomely to convince innocent people to walk through the wrong door.

"Not me!" I said, the sympathetic shopping mom talking to tired, hardworking dad. "I'm immune to all that 'marketing' hooey!"

Hooey? Had I just said the word *hooey*? I had never said the word *hooey* in my life. But it definitely sounded momlike, which was a good thing—for appearances.

Dad nodded. He was antihooey, too.

"Kids like my son would rather have a toy than a piece of clothing with a picture of some toy on it any day of the week!" I said, suddenly realizing that might be true. "What's a nine-year-old boy—my son, he's nine . . ."

Pause. No higher power smote me for making up the kid's age.

"Nine and a half . . ."

Big smile from dad. Mom smile back.

"What's a nine-and-a-half-year-old boy going to do with a sweatshirt with a *picture* of a castle on it? Drive his toy soldiers up the sleeves and attack the collar?"

Dad, supreme guardian of innocent children from evil marketers, laughed. He knew, as (he falsely believed) I did, that the world outside the family unit is oh so cold and often strange. Thank goodness for normal parents like us in it!

"Or maybe he's supposed to hold the sweatshirt over the bathtub and pretend the bathtub's a moat?" he said.

"Whoo boy!" We sighed in unison.

"Well!" I said, realizing that we mothers also use a lot of words that begin with w. *Wow,* and *whoo,* and *well!* I guess they go where all the cursing should be.

"It's been great chatting with you, but maybe I should start with something easier. Like sports."

"There's a sporting-goods store right across the hall from here. They actually sell sporting equipment, not just the clothes. I'd give them a try," dad said helpfully. "And you have a nice day."

"I already have!" I said, realizing that was true, too.

Before I crossed the threshold of the first sporting-goods store I had ever walked into in my life, I took a moment to silently, discreetly read my other little boy's letter outside the electronic doors. Then I walked in.

The first thing I learned was that footballs come in different sizes, just like sweatshirts. There were junior footballs in brightly colored foam and pro footballs that weighed as much as a steak. A lot of them were even labeled "genuine leather," which disturbed my vegetarian sensibilities. Even more disturbing was the fact that none of these footballs sang to me in a way that told me which one to buy.

So I walked up to this very attractive young man in a green sports store vest and said, "I'm looking for a football for my son." He smiled a variation of the security guard smile.

"A football. A football! No way!" he said. "That's gr-r-r-reat! How old is your little guy?"

"Uh, he's eleven."

"*Eleven* is such a great age! I remember, 'cause for me it's only been, like, six years. Where's the kid live?"

"Brooklyn."

"A-MA-zing! I'm *two hundred percent* Brooklyn. Why two hundred? 'Cause *both* my folks were born and grew up here!"

He paused. I laughed.

"So is this Brooklyn boy a Giants or a Jets fan?"

The Undercover Mother in me wanted to ask, Don't the Jets play in New Jersey? But before she made this guy suspect I wasn't really the mother of a football-loving kid, Arty Bike Girl was on the case, flirtationally speaking: "Give us the green one. Green goes great with his eyes!" It wasn't a very sportswomanly answer, but it did the job. Because the salesclerk gently tossed us a Jets football, which, defying the odds and all previous personal experience, I caught.

Then I entrusted him with the second half of my child's letter, the "*or fish*" part. Fortunately, my new friend was a sports polymath, as well versed in the lures of lures as he was in footballs. Frankly, I'd never met anyone so happy with his job. "Now here," he said, barely able to contain his excitement, "is the big daddy of freshwater-accessory knapsacks."

The only word in this sentence I fully understood was *knapsacks.*

"It's power-packed with lures and reels and accessories that are triple A-okay for freshwater fishing!" my new friend explained.

"Super!" I said. "Superdooper!" In my desperate attempt not to sound significantly dumber than I felt, I was smiling so hard, my face was in danger of falling off, revealing the raging fishing ignoramus I'd so blissfully been until then.

Hey! Don't you think we should be getting this kid something vegetarian? Arty Bike Girl says. Just kidding! We're not shopping for us. I know that! Get the knapsack. Go on! I won't say a word. I promise!

Now, a mother shouldn't have a favorite child. But as I was standing in line at the cash register, I couldn't help thinking that I was getting very attached to this little boy. My first letter. He was quickly becoming my favorite child, the apple—no, no, the *football* of my eye. My hope for a happier next generation. He was so friendly and simple, and so easy to shop for. He probably slept through the night from the day he was born. As I fished (Get it? *Fished?* I'm even making Mom-type jokes!) into my knapsack for my wallet, signed the white copy of the credit-card slip and pocketed the yellow, I was indeed one lucky mother.

Next stop? The down jacket.

There was a mother of three coming up from the basement with a big bag of kids' clothing from that kids' clothing store that takes up the whole floor. What a promising sign!

The minute we walked through the door, Arty Bike Girl started running from racks of overalls to boxes full of purple leather hiking boots. She reached for a pair of rhinestone hoop earrings. The Undercover Mother in me slapped her—my—hand. Ouch!

Hey! Arty Bike Girl snapped. Then she sulked her way around the rest of the store, which was packed with everything a little kid could ever need.

For instance, there, on a rack labeled GIRLS' OUTER-WEAR, was an entire rainbow of puffy little girls' jackets. With her high-fashion eagle eye, Arty Bike Girl reached down at the end of the rack and plucked out the one puffy black jacket in a size 10/11 small.

You see! she said. I don't always think that we're "shopping for us," you big grouch. I stuck my arm inside the sleeve. It was puffy but not very warm. And something about it didn't sing to me.

Well, Arty Bike Girl said, maybe what we need is an accessory!

Just then, we saw a table with all these red and black fleecy hats piled on it.

You know, 90 percent of your body heat leaves through your head.

Those hats *are* kind of cute!

Then we were standing in the checkout line, which was half a Brooklyn mile long, offering motherly advice to the man behind us, who wanted to find a hat for his little boy that was as cool as the one we'd found for our little girl. This other mother reached over and said, "You know, I was going to buy my daughter that jacket, but because they're not *down,* they don't keep the kids warm."

You mean we have been standing in line for the last thirty minutes holding a down jacket that is *not* a down

jacket? The only size 10/11 small nondown girls' jacket in this mall and maybe in all of Brooklyn?

What are you looking at me for? I'm only sixteen!

"Next!" the cashier announced. And I could feel an hour's worth of Brooklyn Christmas shoppers standing behind me. Knowing they might riot if I did anything other than pay quickly and let them advance in line, I pulled out my credit card. That's one of my favorite backup plans: When in doubt, charge it. It's an incredibly helpful strategy in those moments when I can't decide whether I'm about to buy the wrong thing or am just too tired to know that I'm holding the absolutely most perfect thing in my hand. And if I'm wrong, hey, that's what return policies are for.

Buying this jacket would also help me in one other area near and dear to my heart: *pride*. I am not a competitive person—okay, I am a *totally* competitive person. Competition in this city is like oxygen: You don't compete here, you die. But while I can handle losing out occasionally to another human—like the day I came in 3,453rd out of 3,500 runners in the mini-marathon I ran last spring, or the time that other woman grabbed the last sample-sale designer dress in our size off the rack right in front of me—I couldn't tolerate being beaten by a mall at this highly competitive game of holiday shopping.

This very *unimportant-looking* building had just blown a big fat retail raspberry at two out of my three kids' Christmas wish lists and sucked every last ounce of energy from my aerobically fit body.

Yes, there is a learning curve in every new undertaking. And yes, I could have given myself a chance to ramp up to speed before I demanded to be victorious.

But that day, I, an expert in selling other people things they don't need, had been denied my basic human right to buy some simple, necessary items!

I had learned there are places that look like toy stores but that sell only clothes with *pictures* of toys on them. Fine, I told myself. Tomorrow, after hours of rest and a bottle of wine therapeutically administered during dinner tonight, I will head to some location as yet unknown to find a three-dimensional castle for a little boy who loves me even though he hasn't met me yet, and never will.

But this nondown down jacket was another story entirely. It was a three-dimensional object in the correct color and size. If I could check the jacket off my list, I would have successfully purchased two out of three kids' presents today. And to my mind, two out of three spelled victory!

So, it wasn't *technically* down. But who was going to know that? I, a professional marketer, hadn't been able to tell that jacket wasn't down when I picked it from the rack!

Okay—I suspected it. But since when did innocence become a crime? Or honesty a virtue?

If my fabulous pseudofriend Tina had been there instead of vacationing at Coppola's hideaway in Belize, she would have said, "Calm down, sweetheart! The jacket you've selected *looks* like a down jacket. Aren't appearances what this season is all about?" Then she'd have gone home, waxed her legs, and headed out to some fabulous party where she'd have fun, fun, fun!

I, on the other hand, bought the hat, the jacket, and the red-gold-and-green-patterned gift box. Then I took the subway home to my apartment, where I lay on the floor of my living room and stared at my ceiling in misery for a seemingly endless amount of time.

One part of me was thinking, Hey. Who would know if I sent this kid a fake down jacket instead of one that's warm? I'm an anonymous Santa!

The other part is saying, You would know. That's who.

I saw myself in a room full of amateur parental stand-ins in some church or synagogue basement in January, confessing how badly I'd failed my child when the holiday chips were down. I saw the banner hanging over our heads. It read NDJBA: NONDOWN JACKET BUYERS ANONYMOUS.

To make matters worse, thirty minutes later, when I left my apartment to have dinner with my good friend Benji in Manhattan, everyone on the street was wearing these enormous down jackets. And looking at down jackets in store windows. And flipping through thick fashion magazines with pictures of down jackets on the cover.

All the way into the city, the windows of the subway keep clacking *real-jacket-fake-jacket-real-jacket-fake-jacket* against the frames. And at every stop, the conductor said, "Change here for DOWNtown! DOWNtown!"

"Why can't everybody just mind his or her own business!" I said to Benji when he answered the door. "I just spent the entire day trying to buy a size ten/eleven small black real down jacket for this little girl I've never met in Brooklyn, and now I find out the jacket's not down!"

"Have a seat on our new imported ottoman," Benji said with his trademark sense of calm. "Taste this pesto Rose bought in the country."

"But it was the only one, and I fought so hard to find it!"

"Hmmmm!" Benji murmured. It's a little noise he makes when he knows he's got things under control, no matter how freaked out we mere mortals might be.

"Have you ever tried to wash a down jacket? You have to put sneakers in the dryer with it—it takes way too many quarters. Have a glass of Oregon merlot."

"Wait!"

"What?"

"But it's not down!"

"Look, if one little kid's jacket is getting you so upset, maybe you're not cut out to be a mother."

"*What?*"

Benji made his little *Hmmmm* sound. "Dice this Vidalia onion—maybe you are."

When I got home, I called my friend Gale, who's from the same place outside of Philadelphia I'm from, which is probably why we say all the same things.

"Does it really matter that it's not a down jacket?"

"You're not rich—a down jacket could cost you hundreds of dollars."

"But what if I give her the fake jacket and she's cold?"

"Oooo, yeah. What if she's cold?"

"So what do I do?"

"Yeah. What do you do?"

That night, I did what any normal New Yorker in my position would do. I obsessed. Wildly. And not just about the normal things. Like: Have I been invited to enough corporate and noncorporate holiday parties to feel professionally successful and interpersonally popular? Or: Would the nonsectarian greeting cards I'm sending to clients and friends have more holiday oomph if I mailed them in frosty, semitransparent vellum envelopes or in traditional green ones?

I didn't worry about whether the snowfall to date meant that skiing would be good this year and I should really reserve a weekend at that adorable, but not *too* adorable, lodge in Vermont. Or whether skiing was passé and it was now time to try snowboarding.

Instead, I spent half the night wide-awake and worrying about shopping for my kids, and the other half having shopping-related nightmares. Hiding under the covers in the overheated dreary dark of my apartment, I dreamed I was racing down fluorescent-lighted hallways into acres of crowded fluorescent-lighted stores. Each store had an enormous picture window with a huge poster that read WE DON'T SELL WHAT YOU NEED! Around every corner, trombone sextets were playing free-jazz versions of carols in an increasingly minor key, like Bach on a very, very bad day. Only the players weren't human; they were . . . they were Heat Miser, the villain from *The Year Without a Santa Claus* special I stopped watching years ago. I screamed, and they started chasing me through ever-repeating mall hallways.

I can't believe it, I thought when I finally woke up. I'm having nightmare reruns!

As the seasonally delayed dawn approached, I was chasing a dream-goose, whose down I would pluck—vegetarian principles be damned!—and shove into a jacket I'd make at home from designer pillowcases stitched with unwaxed mint dental floss. As the garbage trucks outside my window began their daily urban reveille of grinding gears and screeching brakes, I swore that if I could just fulfill my kids' lists, I would never ask for a Real Christmas again.

It was just like the deals I used to make with God after drinking too much warm beer at those jock parties I'd go to with my boyfriend, the adorable, highly alcohol-tolerant coxswain of the varsity crew. I always swore I'd never drink again if He'd just stop the room from spinning this one time—and me from throwing up. My oath about Christmas was that feverish—and just as nonbinding.

I dragged myself from my bed and headed into a day that was as gray and depressingly low-ceilinged as a 1970s suburban basement. I was going straight to the mall. Not the new mall. I was going to the ten-block-long, outdoor, cement, bus-clogged, slightly bankrupt, "largest number of items sold per square foot in America" mall—right there in Brooklyn—a mall as big as the town I grew up in. And I was going to buy a castle and a 100 percent washable real black down jacket if it killed me and everyone around me. Oh yeah, and I was going to do it all before lunch.

Because now I understood. Being Santa is not some "Kumbaya" thing. It's about being Hercules. Only the strong survive.

To add to my holiday merriment, as I turned the corner, it began to rain. Not enough to need an umbrella. Not enough to give me an excuse to stay inside. Just enough to dampen my spirits that extra fabulous mile.

To raise them a bit, I picked up a three-pound bag of Hershey's Kisses in red and green foil at the pharmacy just outside the gates to hell, where a sign wrapped in torn tinsel read WELCOME TO AMERICA'S LARGEST-NUMBER-OF-ITEMS-SOLD-PER-SQUARE-FOOT OUTDOOR MALL!

The first toy store I saw had no name. Just a handwritten sign on a dirty window that said WE SELL TOYS. And a sign on the door that said WE TAKE CASH. And a sign inside the door that said CHECK ALL BAGS. So I walked up to the bag-check guy, who was 50 percent chest hair and 50 percent attitude, flashed him my letter, and said, "I'm looking for a castle. . . ." And the guy leered at me and said, "Hey baby, how about a prince instead?"

All that pomaded hair. All that sleazy attitude and half-unbuttoned green-and-orange polyester shirt atop distressed brown leather pants and motorcycle boots. In a flash, Arty Bike Girl abandoned the state in which we'd been living for the last few days—Abject Misery, Brooklyn—for Total Crush City.

Wow, she said to herself, gazing at her reflection in the guy's shiny shirt. I bet he loves to go dancing! But Undercover Mother wouldn't brake for hormones.

Young lady! she said. We are not here to shop for him!

So I checked my knapsack and showed the letter with the castle on it to this woman who was waiting at the bottom of the stairs; she looked like she'd been waiting down there for the last billion years. Her hair was dyed "Cosmic Hole" black and pulled into a ponytail so tight, it yanked the deep wrinkles that should have been around her mouth to somewhere behind her ears. Her cardigan and lipstick were the same bilious bright pink; her shoes orthopedic; her cigarettes menthol.

She was one very scary lady. And this was one very scary store.

"Everybody says they want a castle," she cackled,

reaching for a cig as she glared at the NO SMOKING sign. "But no one comes here to buy! I tell them, 'Look at this black-and-gray castle with the bloody body parts in the moat. And this purple castle with the unicorns.' So much nicer, even for boys.

"But all the other mothers, they just go to that fancy toy store across the street. But I know you're different. You're the kind of mother who knows a real castle when you see one. You believe me. We discount. We gift wrap . . ." Arty Bike Girl wondered if this poor Scary Toys Witch worked on commission.

But Undercover Mother, that heartless capitalist, told her, Let this be a lesson. You stock quality goods, you get good sales, young lady. And we—

I know, I know! Arty Bike Girl muttered. We are not here to shop for her!

Two minutes later, I was fighting for a yellow-and-orange castle with every mother in that fancy toy store across the street. I've never been pregnant, but as I waddled into the checkout line, I got a sense of what it's like to fight a crowd with an extra-large package attached to your abdomen.

As I waited in line with all the other mothers in Brooklyn for the next ninety minutes, all I could see was the look on my little boy's face as he opened this gift on Christmas morning. How my little boy would somehow know that Santa had been very, very tempted to buy him the castle with the bloody body parts in the moat. But she hadn't. Oh no! Because Santa had bought him a yellow-and-orange castle with—a gigantic gash in the side of its box!

"Don't pop an artery, lady!" the cashier said. "Go back upstairs and just find a perfect one!"

Okay. Maybe Hercules—or a better *tzedaka* Santa—would have done it. But I had a little girl's down jacket to buy. And I had only so much time—and sanity—left. I was no longer in the "frills" section of this project. I was up on the terrifying high wire, where basic items might not be found!

I wasn't playing favorites; I was just being practical. A little boy can live with a hole in his castle box. He might not even notice it. You know how boys are. But a little girl in a fake down jacket is *cold.* And there's nothing like a cold kid to say Santa's lost "his"—"her"—*my*—ability to do things right. These were no longer letters we were talking about. These were my children, and I would deploy every aggressively creative thing I'd learned in this city to make their every last wish come 100 percent true!

(Have I mentioned that there were only four shopping days until Christmas? And that wasn't counting the time it would take to get each of these gifts through the holiday mail.)

Okay, I was outside. It was 11:30. Thirty-two degrees and cloudy. Forty percent chance of snow. Which would go so nicely with existing light rain—no, wait. Could it be? Of course it could! Hail, which was now pelting me from on high.

I was limping into the anchor store of the "largest number of items sold per square foot in America" mall. This was the store that was supposed to hold everything together, although everything there seemed designed to pull me apart. The castle had created a box-size bruise on my knee, which throbbed in rhythm to the holiday easy-listening tunes that assaulted me as I rode up the escalator.

My own down jacket had become a personal sauna in the heat. So, yes, by the time I got to the kids' clothing department on the second floor, I was a little less than rational. I saw a black fiberfill jacket and a pink-and-turquoise down jacket, and I started shoving the pink jacket into the black jacket to make a jacket for my little girl that was twice as warm as every other little girl's jacket in Brooklyn.

That's when this friendly saleswoman came running over and said, "Do you need help?" So I asked her if there wasn't a girls' size 10/11 small black real down jacket in a secret closet in the back, on hold for some other mother, who didn't really want it.

"There isn't," the woman said, "black being this year's color in down jackets and it being so close to Christmas.

"But mother to mother," she said, grinning conspiratorially, "the boys' department is *packed* with black down jackets." She made little quotation marks in the air and said, "'Boys' jackets, 'girls' jackets"—she shrugged—"who can tell?"

God bless her retail soul, the woman was right. Somehow, everything in the boys' department was simpler. Which was exactly what I was learning from having boys. There were black down jackets with big fleecy hoods, black down jackets with big flap pockets. I put my arm into the sleeve of one of them. Not only was it as puffy as a down comforter; my arm boiled.

With the adrenaline rush of a climber approaching the summit, I hoisted the jacket from the rack and carried it back to the saleswoman, who was waiting for me by the register. Even my knee was feeling better.

"This 'Boys' small," I said, making quotations

around the word *Boys* with my trembling free hand and adding a capital letter from sheer joy, "it's just like a 'girls' small. Right?"

"Oh no!" the saleswoman said, in horror and disbelief. "In 'Boys',' it's a whole different story!"

My wildly throbbing knee returned with a vengeance.

"How old is the little girl?"

"She's, uh, she's a girls' size ten/eleven."

"Yes, well of course!" the woman said. "But is she this big?" She put her hand inches from the floor. "Or *this* big?" She raised it over her head.

I was busted. Fortunately, Arty Bike Girl believes that when busted, the best defense is belligerence. (It's always been one of my less successful backup plans.)

"She's above average, of course!" I said in a tone that implied the woman had just questioned my kid's IQ, not her height.

"Well," the woman said, deploying the *w* word in a tone that implied she was talking to a total nut job. Which she was. "In that case, you need a large."

O, holy soul of holiday retail! There is *one* boy's large black real down jacket left in the anchor store of the "largest number of items sold per square foot in America" mall that morning. Yes! Yes! Yes!

And I bought it.

As I walked home to my apartment, I expected everyone around me to erupt into a spontaneous Hallelujah chorus. Which they didn't. So I just hummed it to myself.

I spent the rest of the afternoon wrapping each of the boxes in holiday paper as I happily sang along to every carol-playing radio station I could find. I wrote

letters from Santa to each of my children on fake parchment paper.

"*Dear* [child's name]," I wrote, "*I know what a good little* [boy/girl] *you've been and hope you will love your new* [name of gift] *as much as Santa truly loves you. Merry Christmas to you and your family! Love, Santa*"

Then I wrapped each box in post office–approved wrapping paper and sealed them with post office–approved tape.

By now it's 11:00 P.M. a too few nights before Christmas. My friend Nancy, who's got a huge heart, a night owl's habits, and a blue (the official color of Christmas vehicles—at least in my life) used station wagon, drove me to the main post office and told me she'd circle the block while I popped up to the window and mailed my boxes. Then she'd drive me home to Brooklyn.

Ho-ho-ho!

Ha-ha-ha.

In the dark, the post office had changed from a very important-looking building into something even worse. As I revolved through the doors that separate the street from the post office lobby, I saw what the future had in store for me: a never-ending series of lines.

Like the star of Bethlehem, the lights of the post office had drawn hundreds with the promise of deliverance—or at least, a timely delivery. Each mail person's window was besieged by an endless winding path of supplicants bearing packages and letters that *had to be mailed now!*

There were women in African head wraps and young kids in sweatpants, denim jackets, and spotlessly clean hiking boots. There were old men in work clothes, hipsters in outfits that combined four generations of thrift shop chic in awesomely baffling combinations, and the ubiquitous suit people—overworked, overpaid, overtired.

We could have been the photo on some sadistic charity's holiday card—a series of stressed-out faces on the front, with an inscription inside that read *"Why the hell did we ever wait so long to send this stuff out? Happy Holidays! Please send cash."*

But there would be hours ahead in which to sympathize. Right then, I needed to find the shortest-possible line between my packages and a post office clerk.

Maybe there was an express lane for people with less than three kids—or packages? No such luck. And following the laws of holiday physics, the longer I hesitated, the longer all the lines got.

Wait! There was one line that did seem shorter. And then I saw why: It was the line with the Crazy Lady in it.

You know the Crazy Lady. There's one in every queue in the world. The woman in the supermarket who looks totally normal in her striped shirt dress and sensible flats, until she gets three people from the register, when she starts exchanging every item from her cart for something else, just fast enough to keep you from moving ahead of her in line?

The Crazy Lady at the post office looks just like the Crazy Lady from the supermarket, except she's walking in little circles and arguing with herself about which months really have thirty-one days. Giving myself a mental high five for not getting in line behind her, I opted for the next-shortest line, which was only about the length of six football fields. As I secured my place in it, I was flooded with relief. A second later, I was flooded with sweat. The post office lobby had been heated to summer levels of heat and humidity. Waiting there would be like sharing a steam bath with a thousand grouchy strangers.

Down in Boca, my parents were sleeping off the Hanukkah latkes after a wine-enhanced dinner with friends. Upstate, Buddhist monks were still hours away from silent predawn prayers. *Beati loro,* as my Italian friends would say: "How lucky are they."

An hour went by—slowly.

I bet that in some very logical, northern country, post office lines no longer exist. In Stockholm—or Ontario—for example, I can imagine local children doing village dances while the post office employees go around politely stamping customers' packages and offering tiny cheese snacks along with itemized receipts.

After a few minutes of postal heat treatment, the only thing keeping me from falling asleep on my feet was the nagging pain of the overburdened twine around each package slicing into my fingers. Actually, it was starting to feel kind of comforting.

Just as I was losing consciousness, the post office delivered a rousing Sensurround wake-up call. A skinny white woman with an African head wrap and a long batik skirt jumped out of line a couple of rows down and yelled, "HA!" and started flapping her arms behind her like a bird. "HA!" she screeched as she flapped her way over to the line next to hers, where she again shrieked "HA!" mere inches from a now-terrified man's face.

Two Crazy Ladies in one set of lines! A new record in waiting-related torture.

The German tourist in front of me opened his knap-sack, pulled out a camera, and readied his flash in case the dancing woman returned. Think of how much fun this will be to show in Düsseldorf!

The woman in front of him didn't even flinch as Crazy HA! Lady danced by. She was too busy stuffing dozens of designer scarves into dozens of international express mail envelopes. When each envelope was stuffed and sealed, she attached a preprinted address label to it and crossed another item off the computerized list she had attached to a designer clip board that hung from her thick logo-encrusted belt.

BAM!

"Somebody's shooting, sweetheart!" a man said. I don't know what his sweetheart did at that moment, but the rest of us ducked, *fast,* even the woman with the scarves.

With the impeccable logic of a big-city crowd, we believed one of us had chosen to ignore, big-time, the yellow ATF poster asking us to leave our guns at home and was going, as the French might say, *postal.*

BAM!

"At least spare the children!" someone else shouted.

And then I heard the German tourist's voice saying, "It is just some younger boys with heavy boxes."

BAM!

Hundreds of embarrassed, prone postal customers looked above their endangered heads, to see two teenagers with T-shirts that read MANNY'S PACKAGE MOVERS unloading a four-wheeled cart stacked with heavy cartons printed with Santa heads and sleighs on them. Each carton greeted the floor with a ballistic echo.

BAM!

"Cut that crap *out!*" screamed a gray-haired man in an olive drab windbreaker with a U.S. Army insignia on the back.

"HA!" screamed the Crazy Lady, arms flailing as she reached out to embrace the spirits in all four corners of the post office world.

BAM! went the boxes.

"CUT THAT CRAP OUT!" screamed the army man again, even louder.

"Next," a tired voice said from the window I was working my way toward oh so slowly. In the distance, I could see the face of the woman behind the bars that protected her from truly dangerous customers. It was the same mask of distress and resignation I'd seen on cabdrivers at 2:00 A.M.

I could also see the sign beside her now that read THIS WINDOW FOR EXPRESS MAIL ONLY.

As the woman with the scarves pulled out her designer wallet, I realized that I was holding about a month's rent's worth of mail were I to send it express mail. I pride myself on being a very honest person (impersonating three kids' mothers didn't count as dishonest. It was a gray area for a good cause, okay?). But, honestly, after investing close to three hours to reach the front of that line, I had reached the conclusion that life was too short to change lanes now. Come on, I thought. What's one more little touch of holiday dishonesty among friends?

Just as I was working on my creative backup plan—a "spontaneous" look of innocent surprise I was planning to use when I made it to the front of the line—a woman wearing a post office sweater and Santa

Claus hat walked through the line, saying, "This window is for *EXPRESS MAIL ONLY!* I repeat: No regular mail services at this window."

I sighed the long and deep sigh of the damned.

"Tell me about it," the guy behind me in line said mournfully, pointing to the overstuffed manila envelope in his hand. "I'm a CPA. These are my returns, and they're two years late."

"I'm in the wrong line," I said, pointing to my boxes.

"Hoo boy!" the guy said, turning away. "And I thought I had problems."

"A-HA!" The Crazy Lady had made it to the front of her line. She handed the invisible person behind her window a single postcard and a dollar, got her change, turned to the rest of us, bowed, and danced her way out the door.

I wondered if my friend Nancy thought I was dead.

1:15 A.M. Nightly talk shows had ended. Safe under their covers, couples with better holiday-mailing habits were laughing at jokes they'd forget in the morning, turning off lamps on night tables, and going to bed.

Somewhere in the city, a clock chimed twice—2:00 A.M. By then, I'd been staring at the ceiling for a good half hour, pondering the sign above my head.

✉

That," I say to Mr. Canada, "is where you walked in."

Mr. Canada and I smile and watch together as the woman two people in front of me in line pulls out her neatly ordered packages of scarves, then proffers her platinum card to pay for the international express mailing. The card is swiped . . . and rejected!

Before I can stop myself, I'm gleefully shouting, "Serves her right!" Call me a sadistic Santa, but it feels so great to be in the real spirit of the season finally and watch somebody else suffer, for once. She'll go down in his-to-ry, that scarf woman will! Teach her to double-dip at Gucci so close to Christmas! Maxed out her platinum card sending expensive gifts to people who probably will return them for international store credit, did she? Boo-hoo-hoo!

On the second swipe, the woman's transaction, all four digits of it, is approved.

"I'd love to do *her* taxes," the CPA behind me says.

There is no justice in this unjust Christmas world.

"Next?" the woman behind the counter says.

My hockey honey offers to help me carry my boxes those few feet, but I tell him I'll take things from here. I'm in the final few steps of a twenty-year marathon. I want to cross the finish line under my own power. It's a point of pride.

It's amazing how long it takes to push three boxes across a foot of floor when everyone behind you is wishing you were already gone. Sweaty, and misting from emotion, or the heat—it's hard to tell—when the woman asks me for what I'm mailing, I hand her the box with the football and fishing gear. And the box with the castle. And the box with the first down jacket. I can already picture them gliding down the ramp to wherever boxes in the office go.

"Return address for insurance?" the woman asks without looking up from her postage meter.

"North Pole?" I say.

She looks up and smiles.

"You want to know something? I answer as many of

those letters as I can," says the woman—Mrs. Green, according to her name tag, but she says, "Call me Evelyn! My children and I go out and shop for them together every year! That is the real point of Christmas, the kids!"

By now, the hundred people behind me are convinced that I'm the new Crazy Lady in their line. But to Mrs. Green, I'm golden.

"I didn't know this was an express mail line," I whisper.

"Of course you didn't—they type the signs so small!" Mrs. Green—Evelyn!—says, Santa to Santa, as she weighs my packages and rings me up.

The total seems awfully low, even for regular mail. And that's what I start to say, but Evelyn's giving me the "Sshhh!" sign that tells me she is the adult in charge here. She punches a code into her meter and pulls her half glasses back on top of her head.

"Do you think the boxes will make it by Christmas?" I ask.

"They will *now*!" Evelyn says, and shows me the express mail stickers and postage she's put on my packages. Using some kind of postal worker discount? At her own expense? She doesn't give me a second to ask. "Merry Christmas. Please step aside," she says. "Next?"

Beata sono io: "How lucky am I."

Merry Christmas right back at you, Mrs. Green—Evelyn—times a million. Now all I have to do is find Nancy and introduce her to the love of my life. I wonder: Will it be his place or mine? We haven't had a chance to, you know, talk about *us*.

⊠

I race back to Mr. Canada to let him know that I'll come back for him in the morning, after he's had time to get his passport forms in order. Say around 10:00 A.M.

By the way, I'm going to ask him, after I tell my parents about us, what do you think about a January wedding?

As I run toward what I envision as his open and waiting manly hockey-playing French-Canadian arms— we'll have kids, perhaps—our own hockey team!—the man of my dreams introduces me to an equally hunky blond man in a sensible fur-lined ski coat perfect for cold Canadian winters.

The new man is carrying an envelope with his American passport and his birth certificate in one hand and a clear dry-cleaning bag with two men's tuxedos in it in the other.

"This is the nice young lady who has been entertaining me with her stories about the American Christmas!" Mr. Canada says.

"Hi! Hey—nice formal wear. Somebody getting married?" I quip.

"You got that right!" the blond man says, and grasps Mr. Canada's lovingly outstretched hand.

They have been commuter-relating for too many years, Mr. Canada explains. "But later today, we will exchange our vows in front of a small group of our closest family members and friends."

(Three hundred and fifty of them, as it turned out. I cried when I saw the photos they sent me a few weeks later in the mail. It was such a lovely wedding. The

goalie gave away the groom. I'm sure you saw the paparazzi shots in the papers, or on TV.)

"Sorry to be so late getting here," blond Mark says, "holiday traffic's been terrible, even at this hour!"

"*Pas de problème,*" Mr. Canada says. "We have had such an amusing time!"

Then he shoots his betrothed a smile whose true-love power puts the ones he's been giving me into platonic Canadian perspective. And scores, from the heart. "But even if I had been cold and alone here," he says, "I would have waited for you all night."

"Happy Holidays!" we say. "So nice to have met you! Best wishes on your wedding! *A bientôt!* Bye!"

A truly beautiful story with a happy ending—for everyone except me.

✉

What did I expect? It's Christmas, after all.

But Christmas isn't done with me yet.

If I believed in reincarnation, I would have to wonder if I'd kicked a puppy—a very tiny, defenseless, adorable puppy—in a previous life. How else do you explain something so totally unjust yet *me* as what happens next?

The next morning, I'm taking a walk in my neighborhood, thinking how for a cold day in December, things feel awfully fine. I'm saying hello to my neighbors and people on the street. I smile these warm, spontaneous smiles at little kids on the sidewalk. And you want to know something? They smile back. They can see I'm a real honest-to-goodness Christmas pro! One who's going to get herself a nice hot chocolate at the diner . . . .

Golly gee gosh. Now would you look at that.

A beautiful little boy and his father are going into the diner right in front of me. They're talking. The father is reaching down to take the little boy's hand as they walk through the door. I see the boy is wearing a black down jacket. He's part of this community I've entered by becoming a *tzedaka* Santa to a little girl in another part of Brooklyn.

And on the bottom of his jacket, stamped in big white letters, the way you see things stamped on the bottom of football players' jackets, are the words FIRST DOWN.

Sucker! Arty Bike Girl says: It wasn't a "first" down jacket; it was a *brand*! All that kid wanted was this year's *brand* of down jacket. You just don't understand kidspeak anymore. A First Down jacket! Get it? Get it?

Undercover Mother tries to ease the shame: Well, at least the little girl will be warm. . . . But all I can see is my little girl opening her present on Christmas morning. I see that look on her face—that Suzie Homemaker Oven look—and I hear her saying, "There is no Santa—I didn't ask for this!" Because that's all that kids notice: which things are right, which ones let them fit in.

And the fleecy lined hood, the elasticized sleeves, all the things that made the jacket sing for me back in the mall from hell are now the labels that label me: Giant massive geek. I'm being dissed by some little kid in my borough. I've been too uncool to be Santa.

At this point, I'm ready to resign from Christmas forever. But as I said, Christmas isn't done with me yet.

Just as I've accepted my inner failure as Santa, Tzufen, my former college roommate, whose name means "good fragrance" in Chinese (and great friend in real life), leaves a message on my answering machine. I had told her and her boyfriend, Lars, about my experiences with Operation Santa Claus a few nights ago over dinner. And now Tzufen and Lars want to know where they can pick up a couple of those Operation Santa Claus letters, because they'd like to send presents to a few kids in need of an undercover Santa.

And all of a sudden, the whole thing makes sense.

From Thanksgiving through Christmas Eve every year from now, I'll tell my story about becoming an "undercover Santa," bumps and all, to friends and friends of friends and, eventually, total strangers at holiday parties and in theaters. It'll be a personal *tzedaka* Christmas marketing campaign, whose goal is to get as many people to answer Operation Santa Claus letters as possible. What I'm hoping is that people will spread the word to people they know, like that old shampoo commercial with Farrah Fawcett in it—remember? The first person tells two people about this great new thing she's discovered, and then those two people tell two people . . . and before you know it, the whole world's clued in about this one particular thing.

And yes, the point of this story is that in one way, I, your basic obsessive New York success freak, failed. And yet, maybe not.

Because even though I got my little girl a Suzie Homemaker kind of black down jacket instead of the Easy Bake cool kind, I know firsthand, having been a kid who got the wrong gift from Santa all those years ago, that the most important thing about December 25 when you're young and dependent on the kindness of supposedly more mature people is knowing that someone cares about you on Christmas. Brand names, schmand names. No matter how flawed Santa might be in real life, no child should have to wake up on Christmas morning without a present.

Epilogue

Call me crazy. But every year, I hear another amazing story from someone who's given Operation Santa Claus a try.

The year after I went over to his apartment all freaked out about my nondown down jacket dilemma, my friend Benji took home an Operation Santa Claus letter.

A few days later, he called me, totally freaked out. This is a man who never loses his cool, whether he's cooking a soufflé for twenty or saving a sailboat from capsizing. Instead, he makes his little *Hmmmm* sound.

"You have to help me!" Benji yelled. "I think I'm a racist. I just got back from trying to buy my little girl a doll, and I couldn't decide if I wanted to buy her a black doll because I'm black, or because, from her name and address, I think she's black, or just because it was the most beautiful doll I'd ever seen!"

He paused for a second.

"Hmmmm!" Benji murmured, question answered in the asking.

"What kind of wrapping paper do little girls like better?" he asked. "Hearts or flowers?"

The same year, my friend Gale decided to buy a month's worth of food for a family, in response to a letter from a little boy asking Santa for a warm Christmas meal for him and his dad. On her way through the supermarket, Gale bumped into a young woman who worked there, and showed her the letter.

"It looks like it's from a Spanish family," the woman said. "I'm from a Spanish family, too. I can show you exactly what to get."

The woman led Gale up and down every aisle of the store, filling her shopping cart with beans, pork, oil, biscuits, and plantains. As Gale waited in the checkout line, her new friend called the phone number on the letter to make sure someone was home. "We have a delivery from Santa!" she said. And everyone in the store smiled.

A teenage boy from the store volunteered to deliver the food. It all seemed too good to be true. Was it? After all, Gale thought, this was New York. So she followed the delivery guy around the corner and watched from the shadows as he rang the bell of the apartment where her little boy lived. A few minutes later, the delivery guy and his empty cart left the building, and a little boy stood smiling and waving at an apartment window on the third floor. Gale started to walk west toward the subway, and then looked back for a second. At that moment, the guy from the delivery store, who was walking east, looked back and gave Gale an okay sign, and a nod. Santa had delivered.

Hailey and her husband, Natalio, are artists who live in a cold-water flat in the East Village. They answered an Operation Santa Claus letter from a family of six, who came from the Dominican Republic. They chose this letter because Natalio's from the Dominican Republic, too, and he says no matter how little money he and Hailey have, it's more than a lot of families from back home will ever have.

With the practiced eyes of painters, and an artist's limited budget, they shopped for all six kids, buying knockoffs of designer fashions that were sure to please the kids, and CDs from neighborhood musicians who were the first word in hip. They also bought a few small gifts for the kids' parents to remind them that Santa loved them, too.

On Christmas Eve, they went uptown and spent the night celebrating with their Operation Santa family. It had been hard to contact them, since the parents, factory workers, had only recently found the cash to have their phone turned back on.

Hailey, who volunteers as a high school tutor in her spare time, offered the kids advice on their homework and getting into college. Despite the lack of amenities at home, and the time taken from their studies by after-school jobs, all six children were honor students. A very Merry Christmas was had by all.

✉

Through Operation Santa Claus, I also got to know some of the incredible people at the post office who make this annual volunteer program happen.

Richie is one of them. A very observant Jew, he's a letter carrier who works out of the Murray Hill Post Office. Every December, like so many other amazing postal men and women I've met over the years, he donates his time at Operation Santa Claus headquarters, in addition to doing his regular duties at the post office. There, he helps potential *tzedaka* Santas find the letter that sings to them. He calls himself "the Hanukkah Elf."

One year, while paging through Operation Santa Claus letters during a rare moment of downtime, he found a letter he couldn't put back. It simply asked Santa for a tree.

That afternoon, with a Christmas tree on his shoulder, he returned home to the apartment he shares with his mother. *What is that?* Richie's mother asked, looking at their menorah with its blue-and-white candles neatly arranged for the night.

Richie showed her his letter.

"Wait here," his mother said, then grabbed her coat and left the apartment. An hour later, she returned, weighed down with a huge bag of ornaments.

"Now we can go," she said.

The thing Richie remembers most about dropping off Santa's tree is how surprised and happy the family was who received it. Their home was immaculately clean, he said. But he will never forget that the Christmas table was covered with newspaper because the family could not afford a tablecloth. When she saw the table covered in newspaper, Richie's mother turned to him and asked him for some *kesef*—money—which she gave to the family so they could buy not only a tablecloth, but food to put on it.

I so associate Richie with his Operation Santa Claus role that when I saw him in the spring getting out of a mail truck on Lexington Avenue, I ran over to say hello and ask him what he was doing so far from his official headquarters.

"Delivering the mail," he said, pointing to his overflowing bag on wheels. "What do you think elves do during the rest of the year?"

✉

While most of the people I know do Operation Santa by way of tzedaka or anonymous giving, here's proof of the power these gifts have to change children's lives.

Currently, 14 million American children live in poverty. In New York City, the figure is one child in five.

When I get on a subway packed with kids and realize that one in five of them might not have enough to eat, much less a toy, their faces don't look like statistics; they're kids, rumbling under the streets of one of the richest cities in the world.

It's even more astounding to realize that there are entire classrooms and schools, like PS 279 in the Bronx, where almost 100 percent of the students live below the poverty line. Not that you'd ever know it by visiting. The building, which sits in the middle of a neighborhood where children are not allowed to carry their Christmas gifts home during the day for fear of mugging, is beautiful. The hallways are filled with children's art. The royal blue curtains in the auditorium were sewn by parents' hands.

On the staff of PS 279 was a teacher named Ellen McGovern, who makes sure that each of the school's 750 students receives an answer from Santa to his or her Christmas letter. In addition to her full-time job teaching kids in crowded classrooms, she has kids of her own. In her free time, she devotes herself to a one-woman outreach crusade to draw attention to Operation Santa Claus—in particular, to encourage companies with caring hearts and strong budgets to adopt a classroom's worth of letters.

Ellen told me this Operation Santa Claus story.

Several years ago, there was a boy named Victor in Ellen's class. He was sliding from being a child at risk of failure to a child lost to bad behavior and hopeless grades. Victor's mother was on permanent disability. His father was in jail.

Three weeks before Christmas, Victor wrote to Santa, asking for a warm winter coat. Two days before

Christmas break, the coat came. From that day on, Victor changed.

He wore the coat to school every day, where he never let it out of his sight. He kept it on his chair, refusing to trust it to the coatrack. He took it to the boys' room, to gym, and to lunch. He began to smile. His grades improved.

By spring, Victor was safely in the achievers' section of his class.

"It sounds like such a simple thing," Ellen says. "But that coat was better than gold to him. It showed him that someone out there really cared. My greatest hope is that Victor grows up to become the kind of person who someday can help a kid like he was. Because for a child, that caring makes all the difference."

And not just for the kids.

As I was busy recruiting people to host "*Tzedaka* Santa" holiday parties at their homes and offices last year, I bumped into a guy who had just gotten involved in the residential real estate business. He felt guilty about his job, as landlords are usually the ultimate bad guys in the drama of affordable housing. The ones who raise rents and break leases in favor of making an extra buck, forcing less well-paid, nonsuit types to seek shelter far out of town.

This man wasn't that kind of real estate guy, he swore, but he felt bad about being a new member of a profession that had such a historically evil reputation. So when I told this kindhearted and success-obsessed man that he should host a *Tzedaka* Santa party in one of his apartments, he said yes immediately. (Although he claims it was really just a way to get my phone number.)

In December, we celebrated our first Christmas

together by gathering our friends for a wine-tasting and holiday storytelling party where everyone was invited to take home an Operation Santa Claus letter. On his way to our big event, my boyfriend (let me just say that one more time: *my boyfriend!*) got stuck on the subway. He arrived late and was seriously worried that he'd held up the festivities. "Don't worry," I told him, honestly repeating one of my favorite post office lines, courtesy of Mr. Canada. "Even if I had been cold and alone here, I would have waited for you all night." *

But for me, the most surprising part of this story about undercover giving is that I got invited to my first Real Christmas dinner the year that I first got involved in Operation Santa Claus.

My aunt, who's not my real aunt but an old family friend, has an aunt who hosts an incredible Christmas Day dinner, which has been for family members only for as long as anyone can remember. But this Christmas, I was invited.

So that afternoon, I took the train to Philadelphia. As the train headed south, I was thinking about how my New York kids must have opened their gifts by now. They'd seen the castle, the football, and the gift of the wrong down jacket. I hoped the little girl who got it would give Santa credit for doing her best. I hoped she knew somehow that I'd do my best to get things right next year.

The bus from the train station let me out by a school-yard. When the light turned green, I walked across the big white words on the blacktop, which read CHILDREN XING.

---

* We broke up a few months later when I realized he did love real estate more than people, after all. All I can say is: Kumbaya. You were expecting maybe a fairy tale?

My destination was a small brick house across the street with a big green wreath on its bright blue front door.

Before I rang the bell, I took a second to look through the window. I saw my aunt, and her aunt. And my aunt's sons. And her cousin, Cosmo, and his son, Little Cosmo, and his father, Cosmo Senior. And Cosmo's second wife (who we still thought of as his girlfriend, but who actually eloped with him yesterday). And his brother, the undercover cop. And his other brother, the born-again Christian. He wasn't supposed to know I was Jewish, but he would tell me later, "It's okay, because the rose of Sharon is actually a symbol of our Lord."

In just a few minutes, I would walk across the threshold, shake hands, kiss cheeks, and sit down with the rest of my aunt's family at a table that filled the entire living room. My aunt's family and I would marvel at the pasta that took my aunt's aunt three days to make. I'd say "No" to all seven fish courses again—I'm still vegetarian.

After dinner, Cosmo Senior would give a guided tour of the upstairs floor. He'd show us the bedroom Cosmo Jr. slept in when he isn't staying with his girlfriend of the last fifteen years, who's now his wife—although, like I said, none of us know that yet. He'd point out his bedroom across the hall from his wife's, and say, "We haven't shared a bedroom since 1973. 'S'wonderful!"

But right then, as I stood there looking in through the window, the X in the road behind me, a life's worth of unreal Christmases behind me, too, I swore I could see them passing around this enormous plate of warm spinach. I thought about my three kids opening their presents and I began to mist.

And Arty Bike Girl said, You know, I'm kind of hungry. And my inner Undercover Mother said, Then let's open the door and walk in. So I opened the door and walked in to my first Real Christmas, which was everything I had hoped for, and more.

As it turned out, I was right about one fact of Christmas, after all: The longer something takes to get ready for, the more life-altering it can be.

How to Be an Undercover Santa

The following pages contain a brief history of the post office's Operation Santa Claus program. They'll also tell you how you can become an Undercover Santa in real life. I've included tips on how to obtain multiple letters if you'd like to adopt a classroom of Operation Santa Claus kids, or hold an Undercover Santa party.

An Undercover Santa party is a gathering of friends, family members, and/or colleagues who gather at a host's home or office to read through and select Operation Santa Claus letters to answer while enjoying holiday foods and music.

Being an Undercover Santa opens up a whole new set of holiday choices. Some people choose to answer Operation Santa Claus letters on behalf of a loved one in place of giving a more traditional gift; others answer letters in addition to their regular holiday gift giving. Some deliver their gifts in person, while others remain anonymous. The good news is, no matter how you do it, being an Undercover Santa is a simple yet powerful

way to celebrate the season's spirit of generosity. Did I mention that it feels really good, too?

About Operation Santa Claus

Operation Santa Claus was founded over seventy years ago, when workers in what was known as the Money Order Department of the United States Postal Service's main Manhattan post office started answering letters addressed to Santa. Over the years, Operation Santa Claus has become one of the largest Christmas volunteer efforts in the world. Letters are received from disadvantaged kids and families throughout the United States, and occasionally from overseas.

In 2001, Operation Santa Claus received over 400,000 letters. Approximately one-third to one-half were answered.

Thanks to the generosity of the individuals who answer Operation Santa Claus letters, miraculous things have occurred: Families have been reunited, lifesaving operations have been funded, and a pure belief in Santa has been restored to children who might otherwise have no Christmas. Still, the number of letters continues to exceed the number of givers by almost two to one.

Many post offices around the country have Operation Santa Claus programs of their own. Each program operates independently. To find out if a program exists in your area, you'll need to contact your local post office.

If your post office doesn't have an Operation Santa Claus program, don't panic! You can call Operation Santa Claus headquarters in New York City to have letters sent to you by mail. Since the New York Operation Santa Claus program is the final destination for letters from around the country, you may be able to answer a letter from your area! To receive a letter by mail, call 212-967-8585.

Operators at the main Manhattan post office can also answer questions about Operation Santa Claus and help larger groups and/or interested companies connect with schools that have kids in need. For questions, or to arrange for your organization to answer letters in bulk, call the number listed above.

About Letters

If your local post office has an Operation Santa Claus program, go there and pick letters for your guests in person. Give yourself a couple of hours if you plan to select the letters one by one, *tzedaka* Santa–style. If you're hosting an Undercover Santa holiday party, a good ratio of letters to guests is 2:1. Many people will take home more than one letter for themselves, family members, friends, and colleagues. *Return any unanswered letters to Operation Santa Claus immediately so that other interested adults can answer them in time!*

An important note: As you read through the letters kids write to Operation Santa Claus, you will notice that some children simply ask for one small gift for a sibling who might otherwise lose faith in Santa, while others request expensive items—or lists of expensive items!— such as video games and computers, or high-fashion clothing and sneakers.

While you may feel overwhelmed by or even resentful of letters from kids in need who ask for these kinds of top-dollar gifts, please don't automatically put these letters back, assuming that a child's request is "all for nothing." Children from families that struggle to put food on the table share the same outlandish wish lists as kids whose families want for nothing. They watch the same television commercials and music videos. They have the same designer label–bedecked heroes and dream of looking exactly like the celebrities in fashion magazines and movies as other kids their age.

As one Operation Santa Claus veteran explains so well, "Kids in need often ask for things that we parents may not be able to afford for our own kids. But the truth is, what they desperately *need* is a warm coat, and they'd deeply appreciate a book or a small toy. It's up to us adults to read between the lines. After all, they're just kids!"

Undercover Santa Parties

Some Undercover Santa party hosts invite their guests to share holiday stories before reading through Operation Santa Claus letters. Others prefer to give a brief introduction about Operation Santa Claus's history and purpose.

The most important thing is to make letters accessible to guests, either on one centrally located large table or on smaller surfaces throughout the room. Some guests may feel overwhelmed by the number of kids who need their help. I remind these guests that they can read as many letters as they like and answer one only if it "sings" to them. There's "no obligation to buy."

It is crucial that an Operation Santa Claus form be filled out for every letter that is taken home, as Operation Santa Claus keeps track of kids whose letters have been answered. That way, duplicate letters from one kid don't prevent another's letter from being answered. The Operation Santa Claus forms also allow the post office to assist frantic Undercover Santas who have misplaced their kids' addresses—a very commonplace event during the holiday season!

All completed forms should be returned to the post office by the quickest means possible, which usually means in person, the same day as your party, or the morning after. If you need to mail your forms, the correct address is:

Operation Santa Claus
c/o James A. Farley Building
Main Manhattan Post Office
421 Eighth Avenue
New York, NY 10199-9998
"Completed Operation Santa Claus Form Inside!"

Questions and Answers

Guests may have additional questions about the letters they're reading, or how to answer them. Answers to frequently asked questions can be found at www.love-santa.com. You can also send questions by E-mail to: questions@love-santa.com.

Please remember: Undercover giving, like love itself, is an imperfect yet wondrous exercise. All is possible, and even probable. Happy Holidays to all Undercover Santas. And to all a good night.

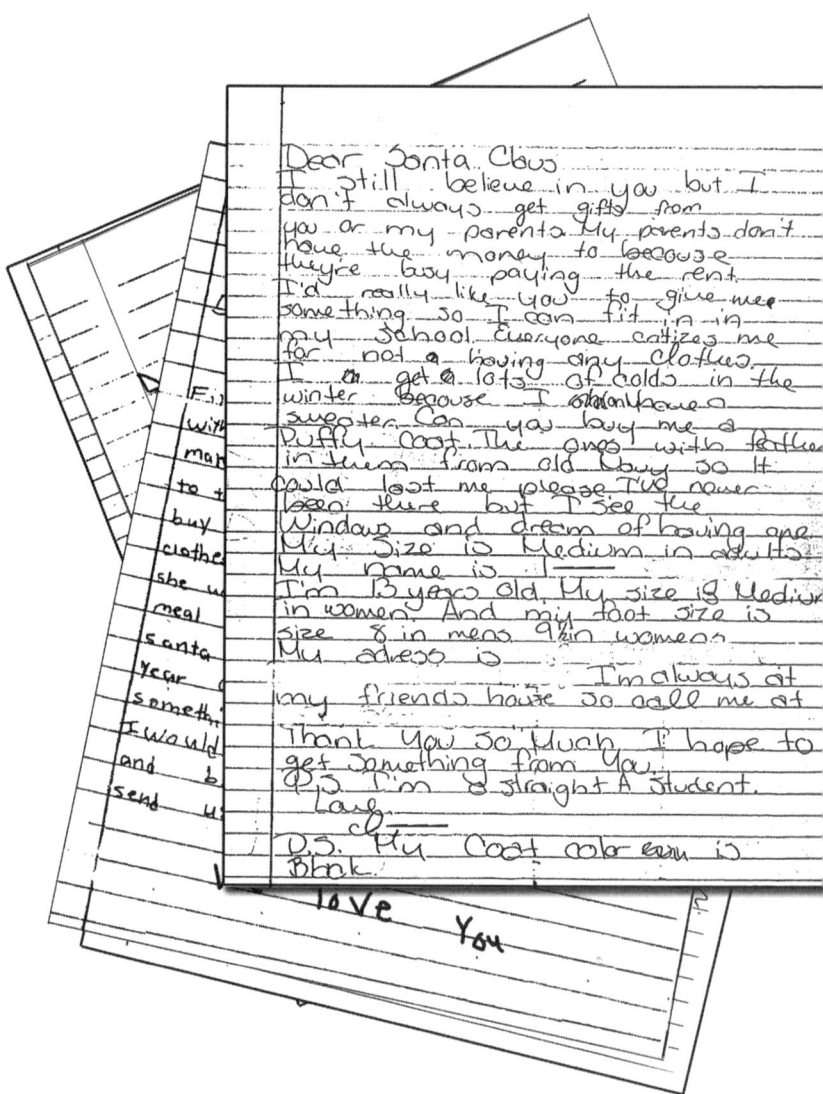

Dear Santa Claus

I still believe in you but I don't always get gifts from you or my parents. My parents don't have the money to because they're busy paying the rent. I'd really like you to give me something so I can fit in in my school. Everyone critizes me for not a having any clothes. I an get a lots of colds in the winter because I dont have a sweater. Can you buy me a puffy coat. The ones with fethers in them from old Navy so it could last me please. I've never been there but I see the Window and dream of having one. My Size is Medium in adults My name is _____ I'm 13 years old. My size is Medium in women. And my foot size is size 8 in mens 9½ in womens My adress is _____ I'm always at my friends house so call me at _____

Thank You So Much. I hope to get something from You. P.S I'm a straight A student. Laer.

D.S. My Coat color can is Black.

love You

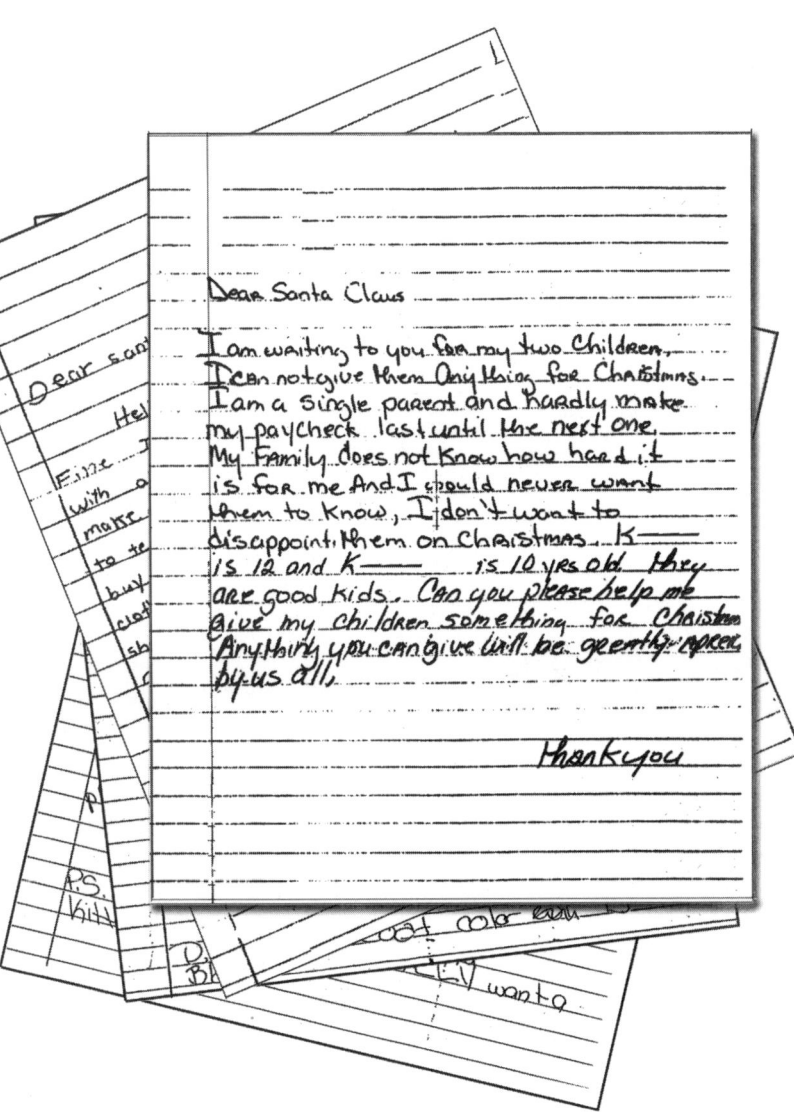

Love, Santa

Dear Santa Claus

I am waiting to you for my two Children,
I can not give them any thing for Christmas.
I am a single parent and hardly make
my paycheck last until the next one.
My Family does not know how hard it
is for me And I would never want
them to Know, I don't want to
disappoint them on Christmas. K——
is 12 and K—— is 10 yrs old. they
are good kids. Can you please help me
give my children something for Christmas
Anything you can give will be greatly appreciated
by us all,

Thank you

Gale Mayron-King

Sharon Glassman is a writer and performer who creates heart-defrosting stories for a high-tech age. For information on Sharon's traveling "Love, Santa" project, or to add your story of holiday giving to her Web site, please visit: www.love-santa.com. Sharon Glassman lives in New York City.